GOD OF THE
SCIENTISTS
GOD OF THE
EXPERIMENT

GOD OF THE SCIENTISTS

GOD OF THE EXPERIMENT

by RÉMY CHAUVIN

translated by SALVATOR ATTANASIO

BALTIMORE, 1960

HELICON PRESS

Library of Congress Catalog Card Number 60-15633

Nihil Obstat: EDWARD A. CERNY, S.S., D.D.
              Censor Librorum

Imprimatur: FRANCIS P. KEOUGH, D.D.
              Archbishop of Baltimore
              October 3, 1960

The *Nihil Obstat* and *Imprimatur* are official declarations that a book or pamphlet is free of doctrinal or moral error. No implication is contained therein that those who have granted the *Nihil Obstat* and *Imprimatur* agree with the opinions expressed.

PRINTED IN THE UNITED STATES OF AMERICA BY
THE GARAMOND PRESS, BALTIMORE, MARYLAND

GOD OF THE SCIENTISTS GOD OF THE EXPERIMENT

For Bergson, who taught me
the "Two Sources"

Contents

Introduction

We will speak here of the God of the scientists and not the God of the sciences. The sciences do not know God, nor do they concern themselves with him. Not because, as is believed by many persons without scientific training, the sciences implicitly consider God as an enemy. It is simply that the sciences look at reality from their own chosen point of view. A great deal of misunderstanding arises because certain scientists look upon themselves as theologians, and too many theologians have never been able to get inside the mind of scientists.

No one understands the mind of the scientist except the scientist: His mind has an amazing lack of philosophical curiosity, it concentrates overmuch on its chosen field of inquiry and knows nothing, indeed has an almost childlike ignorance, of problems that do not concern it directly. Nevertheless this mind is in the possession of Science, one of the rare human adventures that can be said to have been successful to the point that the word "success" can be most perfectly defined in this context. Consequently, whether one likes it or not, the mind of the scientist is shaping a part of the future world. It knows how to handle the most prodigious of human tools, *the experiment*, which can shake the earth, regulate life, and which will soon perhaps achieve its ultimate in imitating the mind itself.

When we speak to scientists we must speak their language, for it is the language of those who are, or will be, the teachers. This is not an original idea, and I also realize that many of the considerations to follow are not new. However, sometimes they do not appear to be new just because of the language. Laboratory people will immediately recognize one of their own in the slogans of the clan, in certain ways of reasoning, and above all in the importance assigned to experiment and the verification of hypotheses. After much reflection, sometimes

1

verging on anguish, it became clear to me that the conflict between the man of science and the man of faith was based on a misunderstanding, and that in reality the scientist could assimilate the faith without repudiating his mentality. Moreover, it is only thus that he will truly understand the faith. This assertion may be disconcerting, but I shall explain it more thoroughly in the following pages.

No doubt this "religion" of the experiment will displease philosophers. It is not meant for them. The author, however, in contrast to his scientific colleagues, has a certain friendship for philosophers. They have been useful as the first integrators of knowledge. But knowledge has moved along much faster than the philosophers. Psychology is now completely out of their domain, and logic requires a long technical preparation. Furthermore, what can a pure philosopher really say now about matter, life, instinct and intelligence? There remains wisdom; that is, the art of regulating one's life. The ancients did not separate this from knowledge. Here philosophers can still have something to say. And since this book is basically a preparation for the eternal search for wisdom, I recognize their right to judge its merits.

I hardly enjoy discussion as a form of combat, but I do believe in an honest attempt to explain the way in which one scientist, out of so many, envisages the problems of human behavior. If the exposition is sufficiently complete, many disagreements fade away and many antagonisms are shown to be absurd. Can the terrible, confusing diversity of opinions—the torment of my adolescence in search of truth—really be reduced, at least to a certain extent? Perhaps the contradictions are only apparent? After all, the different viewpoints one enjoys on the path around the mountain still have to do with the same mountain.

Let us try to place ourselves once and for all in the position of a scientist who feels more or less clearly the incompatibility between an activity ruled by rational techniques, and a moral life that is subject to tropisms; tropisms that are poorly understood, much less discussed in their essence and are under the domination of chance and circumstance, but not of reason. Since his occupation is conducive to meditation, it is impossible that the scientist will not ask himself the questions of suffering, death, the meaning of life, and of God. But he does not ask himself these questions as other men do; he cannot give credence to old wives' tales, nor commit himself blindly to the residues of his early childhood. He has certainly heard it said, and by men of genius like the great Pasteur, that one can divide one's life in two: one, that of the man of the laboratory obeying the inhuman conclusions of the experiment; and the other, that of a mere man who weeps at the bedside of a dead child and who cannot believe that all is now irretrievably over. But this is to reason like a coward: why all these senseless mental acrobatics, this absurd compartmentalization, this permanent preservation of a conflict? This is a big joke! Either science, as the scientist firmly believes, is the only means we have to reach reality, and therefore can be *applied to everything on the condition that it is not hampered by prejudices or arbitrary restrictions;* or else certain domains of reality simply escape science. This represents a serious menace to science which has never known any area locked out to it by definition. It had always ended up in the very center of those areas to which philosophy wished to deny it access. No scientist will ever accept these restrictions. Let us therefore resolutely advance along every possible way, but let us first rid ourselves of some unconscious philosophical residues which could block the investigation.

First of all there is question of the "moral" world, as it is commonly called. What is the moral world? What part do intelligence, will, and freedom play in our decisions? In the first place are we not determined by tropisms; are not our "decisions" thus illusory?

In the first chapters it will be necessary to examine the bases of our activity, and to determine how the scientist can understand the great philosophical problems that have been posed in this connection. I do not ignore the fact that my very way of posing these problems might often irritate the philosophers. But in our times and given the active state of science, we cannot deal with will, intelligence and freedom as did Aristotle or even Kant.

Let us suppose that this work of the preliminary clearing away can be accomplished. We shall not thereby claim — an intolerable presumptuousness—to have elucidated the springs of the mind and the act. But we shall better discern the angle from which they must be considered, and we shall at least be able to fix the limits of the obscure zones. Yet we shall still not have discovered the reasons for acting, the rule for living. Men of all times have sought for these reasons in *religions*. Thus it is fitting to examine briefly the religious phenomenon, first in the prehistorical and then in the historical periods. Perhaps we shall then find the means to penetrate further into the motivational mechanisms, by a rapid survey of the panorama of the "theotropic" reaction in time and space. This instinct has evolved considerably. And it still expresses itself in powerful constructs in our time. Then we shall have to consider the great religions. Faithful to our set purpose, however, we shall philosophize as little as possible in order to have recourse primarily to observation. The assertion by a philosophy or a religion that it can guide men, give them stability, and lead them toward a higher kind of happiness must be verified concretely. In the sciences, theories are judged by their effects, and the tree by its fruits. Only two religions seemed to me worth being retained for this examination: Christianity and the Hindu complex. I shall pass over Christianity rather quickly at that point because I shall return to it later in the book where I shall dwell at length on the religion of Brahma, comparing it to the religion of Christ.

But all this is still nothing, or nearly nothing. Observation alone, and the description of religious phenomena, cannot give an answer to the questions we posed at the beginning. For it is not simply a purely intellectual process. It is in the domain of the "physics of the act" that religions are practiced. In order to understand them rightly, it is absolutely necessary to have experienced them. I do not know whether a scientist who is a Christian can deal with the history of religions in a completely impartial manner. But the non-Christian scientist, for sure, is completely incapable of understanding Christianity.

In the second part of this book I will discuss how experimentation is really possible when it comes to religion. And, always adhering to this same method, I will be very careful not to state presumptuously that which I think ought to be, but will content myself with an observation of that which *is*. The phenomenon of conversion will be dealt with before we finish in order to show its termination in contemplative experience in the Christian religion.

When the reader has finished this work I hope he will admit that

I have remained faithful to the law of the sciences, that I have not repudiated the practices of the laboratory. I have perhaps extended the meaning of the term "experiment" more than my colleagues are in the habit of doing. But this was a legitimate extension, and I shall have fulfilled my aim if the reader is convinced of this.

Part I

1

Some Notions to be Clarified as a Preliminary

The scientific mind and the philosophic mind

In order to remain faithful to the spirit of the sciences, I see myself forced to adopt a mode of reasoning here which will irritate philosophers. Working in laboratories has accustomed us to make our minds function in a humble, matter-of-fact manner, with constant references to concrete data. In short, there is more than one difference, in the use of their minds, between the wearers of the white "lab" coats and the Lovers of Wisdom. In particular, the cultivation of ancient masters is completely alien to us. Let us dwell for a moment on this characteristic. It does not lie beyond the scope of our subject. For if the reader does not understand it, he will be even less likely to grant most of the assertions that this attitude will dictate later on.

For example, one would greatly astonish a microbiologist by asking him whether he has read the complete works of Pasteur, or a paleontologist by raising the same question in connection with Cuvier. Most specialists would immediately answer that it's much more important to have a thorough knowledge of the scientific literature of the past ten years, and that they have not read a line of the old masters, even though they admire them as much as you do. Science sets out from the materials of the present without concerning itself with the vehicles which have brought it to the present. Not because it does not know about these vehicles, or scorns them, or denies their usefulness; science simply has no need of them. Undoubtedly this is why so few scientists are interested in the history of the sciences. The historical approach of the philosophers is something profoundly alien to them.

Once again, only the contributions of the most recent years are of importance. And this for the very simple reason that the more ancient works were achieved with antiquated techniques now considered as rudimentary. Now one cannot separate *the results from the technique which served to elaborate them*.

It is the continuous perfection of the instruments of his research which characterizes the approach of the scientist and which to a certain extent differentiates him from the philosopher who practically is still using the same instrument as Plato. This is why, moreover, the philosopher still finds both pleasure and profit in reading Plato. The scientist, on the contrary, is used to a parade of facts, ceaselessly probed, of measurements, ceaselessly more precise, which are being continually and rapidly perfected, and utterly changing the face of the great theories. Consequently, any student of bacteriology today knows more than Pasteur, and does not see why he should waste his time reading the latter's works. He would not even be able to learn how to reason by reading them because in many of the sciences (except mathematics and physics) the reasonings are very simple, even though the experiments are ingenious; but the facts are better and better scrutinized: *the facts, that is, but not the texts*.

Faithful to the practices of the laboratory, even in the investigation of God, we shall first of all pose the *question of the technique* that we are going to employ in this investigation—or, more exactly, of the mental tool which we have to put to work. The question is not simple; it even implies a lighting difficulty which takes account of all that follows. For many it seems evident at first sight that the problem of the existence of God and of the moral law must be solved on the plane of intelligence and there alone; whence arose the famous proofs. I don't believe they succeed in proving the existence of God, but *they do demonstrate very well* that nothing in right reason is opposed to *one's belief in the existence of God, if one wants to believe*. Now, in my opinion, to place the problem on a purely intellectual plane, to wish to demonstrate God like a theorem, is to preclude any results; to lock oneself in the prison of the "undecidables," a term which will be explained later. I believe, on the contrary, that one can advance here, as elsewhere, with the help of experiment, that is to say, with the constant confrontation of a certain part of the mind with the facts. In this way we arrive at more modest and provisional certainties:

the very certainty of the sciences. But we shall never find ourselves stalled before a First Mover about whom one can say nothing save by the *via negationis*. And we shall be able to continue forward and little by little get around many obstacles.

To place the problem of God on the grounds of intelligence only, by means of intellectual interpretations of the world, would also involve a serious inconvenience for the scientist which we can clearly see; namely, that of going outside the domain of the experiment. An interpretation made only in the light of *nous* can always be demolished or canceled out by another. Who can decide if there is no real *method of verification;* that is to say, again and always, a reference to the facts? A theory that is not verifiable does not interest the scientist. The very idea which guided me in undertaking this essay is that if God exists, it must be possible to verify it (not to *prove* it). Or else, if one prefers, belief in an undoubted God produces a reorganization in the moral domain (*which is that of action*) whose effects should be observable. A more elaborate, more perfected belief must act further, it must produce a better equilibrium, exorcise the phantoms of sorrow and death more perfectly, and at the same time (*but this is only one of its roles*) furnish a good interpretation of the world to the discursive intelligence. And the best results (which either an already existing science, or one that will be created, would be able to evaluate) will be necessarily furnished by the truest religion, that is to say, the one that works best on the whole human behavior.

Reality and importance of "moral" facts

Evidently this presupposes that one considers moral facts just like any other fact and that one attributes as much importance to the sorrow of a mother alongside her dead child as to the combination of hydrogen and oxygen. Do not exclaim, "That doesn't follow!" In the mind of a great number of scientists there exists a semi-unconscious but very solid prejudice: the laws of physics and chemistry possess importance only because they can be measured, so that by mixing two well-chosen reagents in a test tube one will always obtain the same red coloration. Changeable as they are in their essence, human facts are therefore viewed only with mistrust. They are almost not facts at all, one does not see how they can be validly dealt with, since one can neither make use of them nor deny their existence.[1] If one grudgingly admits their existence, they will be at least denied any importance. This is why, as I emphasized in the Introduction, so many of our colleagues are giants in scientific knowledge, and eight-year-old children with regard to the motives of their acts. And this is also why there is nothing in common, alas, between science and wisdom, even though the herd is so inclined to believe the contrary.

Such a dichotomy is truly absurd. For my part I cannot accept it! As I shall say later, the scientist cannot so lightly regard that complex of motives (not purely intellectual) which specifically impelled him to become a scientist. Let him repudiate this vain timidity, let him get used to looking upon the "moral" world, as quite as accessible to science as any other world, and let him grant it that title to unlimited importance which it in fact possesses! Science can no longer put off the eternal questions: Who are we, where do we come from, where are we going, what are we doing on this earth, and why?

If we consider man in the world with the cold eye of science, a series of banal statements straightway assert themselves: in order to act, man needs a *reason for acting*. He fears suffering, old age and death, and tries to escape or bypass them. He wishes for happiness or stability and looks for them in all his acts, most often gropingly. Above all he would like to understand the world and what he is doing in it. Consequently a theory or a religion which will fully answer his problems, whose efficacy he could verify every day by putting it to the test, will be true, because it *works* in the "moral" domain. This is as true as another theory which asserts that in order to combine hydrogen and oxygen, a match must be applied. A theory is true when it responds to the nature of things, because it *conforms to the real*, and because there is simply no other usable definition of truth.

Thus, we most certainly are not dealing with the World of Ideas, we do not at all penetrate the empyrean where mathematical certitudes reign. But as the sciences teach us, these ideas are difficult of access

---

[1] This defective reasoning is characteristic of scientists who are inclined to deny what their science does not yet know. Let us not forget that the great Laplace denied the existence of aerolites "because stones cannot fall from the skies, for there are no stones in the sky!"

to us in this world. If this seems bitter to us it is because we have tarried too long with pseudo-problems, as we shall see later.

Complex nature of intelligence

Moreover it must be admitted that the very notion of intelligence is now quite obscure. Is one really sure of what one is saying when one asserts the necessity of considering the problem of God in the light of this faculty? The notion of intelligence, borrowed from Greek philosophy, has been pulverized in our time into an ensemble of functions, probably very heterogeneous, and which we hardly know how to connect. And one cannot get much from it in its traditional form. I may seem to dismiss the sublime pages of the masters of Hellas too lightly. But we laboratory people are convinced that no work, no page is immortal except by reason of its transient beauty. All we do is contribute our stone to the edifice of knowledge, but it will inevitably be capped by others and it will be quickly forgotten. And we are resigned to this, in the asceticism peculiar to the scientist. The origin of the modern revolution in the conception of intelligence starts with the deliberate forgetting of the Greeks and the philosophers who followed them. They did not study intelligence in every conceivable way. They forgot one way: *measuring it*, a task to which we have been devoting ourselves only in recent years. This is not the place to summarize the admirable investigations of the schools of Thurstone and Spearman. Let us just say that the profound study of tests and of their correlations have brought to light enigmatic factors which very often can be designated only by letters and cannot be clearly defined in ordinary language: speed of perceptive structuration factor, the flexibility of structuration factor, the speed of judgment factor, the mysterious "g" factor of "general intelligence," etc. These are all terms that will unquestionably confuse a mind formed only by the traditional disciplines. Whatever one may think of the data of factorist analysis, which still flourishes hardily, it cannot be denied that they make us perceive the extreme complexity of the problem. As soon as one pursues precision and tries to measure, then the *nous* is no longer clearly perceivable, but only an ensemble of heterogeneous faculties bound together perhaps—but this is not entirely sure—by the famous "g" factor, i.e., mental energy or agility.

Research can be done in other directions. Experimental psychologists themselves are preoccupied with finding more general, but above all *operational,* definitions. For Piéron intelligence is confounded with the ability to know how to adapt oneself to new situations. Zazzo thinks that it is the ability to solve problems, to get out of difficulties encountered outside the learning processes. He links the notion of intelligence to that of mental growth. Thurstone and Terman tend to identify intelligence and the power to handle abstractions. Bergson asserts that it corresponds to the undefined power to decompose according to any law and to recompose according to any system. For De Montpellier intelligence is the grasping of new relations of a different type, whence its very different forms and levels. Stoddard claims that it involves a special "ability" in activities that are difficult, complex, abstract, realized economically, adapted to a goal, of social value, involving originality, concentration of energy, resistance to emotional forces.[2]

At any rate all modern psychologists would agree on the fact that the type of intelligence which corresponds, for example, to the solution of moral problems (if it be the intelligence which applies itself effectively to them) cannot lightly be compared to scientific intelligence, to artistic intelligence, etc.; it is simply a very different function, one which we do not know very much about. Let us always keep in mind this notion of *heterogeneous intelligence,* a great bracket which encompasses a whole series of perhaps absolutely independent subjects.

Affectivity and intelligence

We are still able to fall back on affectivity and the will, a group of functions which have full play in human behavior. But we shall not do this, precisely because it would involve ancient notions collected from the ashes of Hellas. It would take much time to dust them off

---

[2]G. D. Stoddard, *The Meaning of Intelligence* (New York: Macmillan, 1944), p. 4.

properly. It would be a difficult task to define them. Moreover, they would cramp our reasoning, because traditionally they are too separated from intelligence.

Is this separation justified? Does the intelligence in the ancient sense of the term, float on the calm sea of the Ideas? Can it be so separated from affectivity? Common sense already warns of the difficulty of the operation. It appears to be possible only in the handling of abstract concepts, like those of propositional logic, for example. But as soon as the concepts are more concrete, and particularly when there is a certain degree of complexity, the inevitable affectivity promptly enters in to tamper with pure lines of abstraction.

Is this not obvious even in mathematics? We need not go as far back as the Pythagoreans who, it is said, drowned one if their initiates who had discovered the irrational number, because it was an affront to the majesty of the One. We have only to recall in our own day, the passionate attacks which drove the great Cantor to distraction. Undoubtedly this is only the expression of overardent temperaments, for whom an abstract argument had a life of its own. In other respects, mathematicians keenly feel the "beauty" of a proposition or the "elegance" of a demonstration. All the same these are emotions that are somewhat out of place in the sphere of Ideas! Undoubtedly, someone will say, but that in no wise changes the correctness of an equation. Precisely! But it does hamper the reception of many pioneers. Cantor knew something about this.

I can speak from memory about physics and particularly biology. Everybody remembers the virulent controversies about evolution, about genetics, about relativity. The fact is that here the great theories were so impregnated with philosophy (for or against) that it was completely impossible for the adversaries to abstract from it. Here, as Socrates observed, everybody philosophizes without knowing it. And it would be better to become aware of it so as to philosophize well.

As a matter of fact, if any one is not convinced of the interactions between the intellectual and affective spheres, I have perhaps an even more powerful argument in reserve: Why does a mathematician, a biologist or a physicist cultivate mathematics, physics or biology? Is it not because these disciplines *interest* him? But what is interest with respect to a science? Can it be defined in strictly intellectual terms? I very much doubt it. To love physics or biology is to have a *feeling for them* powerful enough to inform and imbue one's entire existence.

Motivation

And it is not at all true that intellectuality, affectivity, and volitional inclinations as separate entities are blended in this powerful feeling of which we have been speaking. No, they all belong to that indeterminate zone of *motivation* which predates such categories, which is neither thought, nor affect, nor will in the pure state. Thus what drives the most resolutely intellectualist of our scientists and our philosophers to dogmatize, in a certain sense their entire life, is *something not purely intellectual.*

Should this discourage us? Should we declare that since the foundation of being is a deep-seated irrationality, we must abandon ourselves to the vague drives of instinct? Of course not. Let us limit ourselves for the moment to following the modest course of the sciences, admitting that man is more complicated than one thinks, that "mind" is much more than "reason." One should not complain about being imprisoned, when one has sealed the bars of one's intellectual prison by oneself, and does not want to give it up. We shall have occasion to discuss much valuable information on motivation in the following chapter, in the course of attacking various prejudices.

But we can already take up again the old distinction of the scholastics: the factors of moral conduct must not be sought exclusively in what is represented, *id quod repraesentatur,* but in what inclines to assent, *id quod inclinat ad assensum.* It is true we must admit that we do not completely separate the "represented" and the "assent," and that the verb "inclinat" interests us very much because it lends itself to measure.

Moreover the Vatican Council condemns those who attribute the entire determination of beliefs to reason—and also those who, contrariwise, make everything depend on a kind of inner revelation experimentally perceived. Thus a double difficulty arises when one is locked in the prison of categories. As we shall see, raising walls that are too solid between "intelligence," "affectivity," "will" etc. (all categories that would suffer very much from precise definition) throws oneself *a priori* into inextricable difficulties.

Role of the experiment

In the remainder of this book we will follow the same type of pragmatic reasoning as used in those samples which appeared in the previous pages. I know to what extent this can be irritating for some and I apologize. I do not want to offend them, nor above all to harm them spiritually in any way. But when we are talking about religion and the moral conscience the uselessness of discussions purely on the level of the intelligence can easily be discerned. Who will be convinced? Those who have derived any profit from this sort of thing are rare. At best one only ends up with a notion of which I shall make frequent use—that of the "undecidables"—employing it, however, in a different sense from that of the mathematical-logicians. I am referring to the undecidable character of those questions to which affirmative or negative answers each involve arguments of the same weight. We are very familiar with these problems in the sciences. Our conclusion in the case of undecidables must be always the same: there is an error in method, something else must be investigated, there is a third way of considering the subject. This third way cannot be investigated by reason alone, it must be accompanied by experiments.

For experiment is fruitful; it is indispensable for the progress of knowledge. If theology seems to have been stagnant for so long, is it not because it is too intellectualized? After having agreed that God is experienced rather than proved, theology too quickly forgot that it had recognized the usefulness of experience, and again fell back on abstract reasonings. Now, would it not be possible to imagine a positive theology which would appeal to observation? For after all, according to the great Bergson, humanity has never known the God of the philosophers, nor the Unmoved First Mover, nor the Limit to the *regressio ad infinitum*. These are purely intellectual beings, and humanity proceeds quite in another manner. For mankind God is *Dyaus*, the brilliant sky, but He is also *Dyaus-pitr*, Father, good, just, all-powerful, but who has withdrawn from men.

Now please do not tell me that this is a naturist concept of little interest, the genesis of which can easily be explained (by such things as the fear of lightning, admiration for the vault of heaven, etc.)— and which does not lead us very far. One who says this, knows the history of religions very poorly, and forgetting *"pitr,"* sees only *"Dyaus."* Above all he forgets that the instinctive creations of man can lead us far toward his motivation and tell us that *he has a need to believe in order to act.* Would it be nothing then to understand this need clearly? I shall develop these considerations in the following chapters. But from now on let us not imagine man in too simple a fashion, when animals, as we shall see in a moment, are already so complicated. And let us not believe we know everything about man, when the bases of an *observational theology* are yet to be constructed.

But in the sciences observation cannot suffice, experimentation must be joined to it. I think that the Vatican Council intended to condemn those who wanted the source of faith to be only a certain exalted, para-mystical feeling, and who believed they could discover God only in the effusion of the heart. But this is not the way I understand experience. What I attach the greatest value to *is the verification of the profound correspondence of certain rules to human conduct,* and of the essential lack of correspondence of certain others. Correspondence (and lack of correspondence) can be the objects of internal and external observation, and of experiment. Consequently they allow us at last to emerge from the zone of the undecidables, and to progress.

Up to now theology[3] has not made use of the history of sciences and even less of experimental psychology, which it particularly fears. But, it is necessary to go forward out of the wasteland of mutual misunderstandings; I repeat again, it is necessary to go forward!

Some other notions that must be understood

Since we are going to use or at least imply certain notions continually, it is best to agree immediately about their meaning and importance.

Consciousness, an enigmatic notion, is a singular power through which the human machine knows itself as a machine. According to

---

[3]There is an excellent discussion of this experimental aspect of religious knowledge in *The Christian Experience* by Jean Mouroux.

Leibnitz, if one imagines a watch large enough so that a man can walk around inside it, one will see only wheels driving one another, but nothing that explains the machine conceiving itself as measuring time. This autoreflection is maddening, by itself it undermines traditional materialism, and by itself it would establish the bases of all the audacities of spiritualism. Some have seen this clearly and have called it an *epiphenomenon*, hoping thereby to have rid themselves of it. For, they say, whether autoreflection is present or not there is no effect in human acts. I find in this reasoning the mark of a naïve exclusionism which has done much harm to the sciences. As soon as a phenomenon is found to be embarrassing, it is minimized to the point of suppressing it. This, moreover, serves no purpose because the fact thus despised avenges itself sooner or later. In the matter of knowing whether man without consciousness would still be a man, *I look for someone to make an experiment on it.* At most I grant that few men make very much of their consciousness, and even among those who utilize it, the *intensely* conscious moments remain very rare. Moreover, if consciousness is an epiphenomenon, it still must be explained: it *is* there. . . . One blushes to assert obvious facts of this kind, but perhaps it is not useless. Finally, according to the profound remarks of Piaget, perhaps there exists two distinct worlds, the world of causality and the world of consciousness: Distinct, but *isomorphic* and corresponding to one another point by point, which would explain the fact that one does not find consciousness when one seeks for it on the plane of causalities. This does not mean that it is of no interest to study the plane of consciousness, using its own norms.

Freedom is an even more difficult notion, which really raised the blood pressure of Loeb and Watson. And I shall say nothing about the philosophers for whom the problem of knowing whether an act is accomplished because the motives for doing it are the stronger, or whether the motives are stronger because one has chosen them, has been the subject of endless controversy. But let us not dwell on this because here we have, I fear, an undecidable. For me freedom is like the sight of colors that one cannot define: freedom asserts itself and that's all that may be said. It vanishes as soon as one tries to reconstruct it discursively. Why would one want to discuss the color red, as color?

But if I pass over such a serious subject at such a maddening speed, it is because I am holding in reserve a pragmatic argument which will appear under several forms in this work because it aptly corresponds to the mentality of scientists. Very well, I will admit you are right, adversary: you have neither consciousness nor freedom. You are but a blind aggregate of molecules, subject only to necessary physical laws. Be quiet then! Why argue and try to convince me? My very changes of opinion are themselves necessary and predetermined: why strain yourself? What interest does the controversy have? You have but one right; the right to keep silent since in your view discussion, effort, and even action itself, are by definition absurd.

Consciousness and freedom are notions that one cannot reject by going through to the very end with one's refusal. One can pretend only *not to think about it any longer,* while *acting as if one accepted them.* To deny them is to fall immediately into incoherence, to disassociate thought and action definitively; consciousness and freedom are *laws of the mind.*

Let us accept it, since we cannot really do otherwise. Now let us try to penetrate the motives of free action: these motives will be either more or less lofty. Among most men they barely go beyond the level of conditioned reflexes. But what interests us is action at its highest level: for example the choice of a life's work preceded by a conscious deliberation, or the making of a difficult decision, implying suffering and prolonged effort. Now, in order to promote action, hope must surpass effort: it must be greater than any effort no matter how prolonged and painful it may be. And if what one risks to gain is infinite by definition, no effort, no sorrow, no torture is too great because these are limited in space and time. I shall speak of the meaning of the word reward later, but in the meantime, let it be said that it must not be understood in a strictly juridical sense.

Let us return to the conception of man that can be gleaned from the previous pages: A being imperfectly known in his essence and reactions, whose faculties break the carcan of the categories of the past; with the mystery of his motivation on which everything depends; daring everything in his mind, even mental suicide, but nevertheless unable even to reason except by following certain laws which he imagines to transgress without really transgressing them. Consciousness and freedom figure among these *conditions of discursive thought,* the essence of which, however, escapes his concepts. Thus man is impelled forward toward more truth by an instinct stronger than himself.

Is not this word *truth* itself terribly ambiguous? I would not dare to venture into the jungle of definitions that have been given to it. Let us rather, again and always, follow the approach of the sciences by asking ourselves *which is the most useful*, i.e., that which permits real progress, and that which laboratory people make use of consciously or unconsciously. No hesitations, then! *By truth they understand that which conforms to the real* and which consequently allows action upon it. As we have already seen, a true theory is one "that works," one that inspires successful experiments, that permits a forward march. At a certain moment the flow of new facts causes the old theories to burst. It becomes necessary to invent others that are more true because they explain more facts and allow nature to be modified more surely. And whether one likes it or not we biologists have no other criterion of correspondence to the real than these more or less successful experiments.

Undoubtedly one arrives only at a relative truth in this way. But to believe that the absolute can be achieved *on this earth* is nothing but the prejudice of a young boy, a remnant of one's intellectualist salad days. The knowledge of one's limits should hardly be cause for despair. For one may draw back from them, and find, as the sciences show, an opening pointing toward an immense future. But we must stop wishing to have arrived at the goal, when we have barely started out. We cannot gain access to the real by simply solving an intellectual equation which will then reveal the whole of reality to us. The mind, under pain of sterility and tautology, cannot base itself only on the mind: this is a chimera of the philosopher! It requires a fixed touchstone, which we call the external world, in order to verify its concepts. One gains access to the real only little by little, by the action and reaction of the world and the mind. And what is so sad about that?

Some conceptions, valid and otherwise

This idea of a morality handed over (in part) to science is not new, but there is more than one way of understanding it. I cannot agree with one of the proponents (save on one point), repelled as I am by some diverse, rather major, paralogisms. I would like to deal briefly now with Bayet and his scientific morality.

The idea that science is going to produce a morality or that morality will depend on science is very widespread among the general public and especially among Marxists. I have made many efforts to understand just what they are trying to say and I am afraid I never shall. Thus, confused by my lack of understanding, I would not have discussed it at all had I not from the start seemed to discern therein monstrous philosophical presuppositions passing themselves off as objective science. When Bayet declares that "the role of science in the moral domain does not consist in finding the guiding rules of activity, but to study moral reality, that is to say moral facts and their laws," I am entirely in agreement! But then the gallant gentleman continues: "As the science of morals develops further, revealing unknown realities, it will become possible to fashion a scientific morality, that is to say to constitute a rational moral art capable of acting deliberately and effectively on moral facts." Thus, we pass surreptitiously from the descriptive to the normative plane. For science cannot *act* on phenomena except with the aim of achieving a determined effect. Now, who is going to assign science an aim? I understand very well that science does not need one if only experiments must be made, for example, to determine precisely in what sense a moral decision would be influenced by a given situation (which besides would be very interesting). But next comes the transition to the normative, "The moral art . . . will eliminate what in it no longer conforms with the sensitive feelings of the common conscience. It will substitute therein ideas . . . which, contained in embryo in this conscience, await only an intervention of this kind to blossom forth and bloom." Here then the norm is confused with common conscience and the ideas developed therein, the whole being considered as good ("good" in the Platonic sense of the word, toward which it must aim). I can hardly discuss this concept of the common conscience. One would first have to ask oneself whether it is really conscience and whether it is common. And whether at the time of Roman decadence, for example, it was good to follow the common conscience, provided that it existed, etc. But further on he writes: "The proper object [of practical morality] is to improve moral reality. Let us improve our knowledge of the real, let us turn it into account in order to create a little happiness . . . In morality, progress will consist in finding combinations better adapted to the common interest." Now it is the common interest that becomes the highest norm. What are its relations with the common conscience? In short, in all these notions I see only a very vague magma which becomes completely liquid as soon as one looks for some element that is a little bit solid.

Science, let it be said once again, can prompt nothing but experiments and make combinations among them. It will never tell you whether it is good or bad to undertake them, but only whether or not there is a chance for success. On that day in the Nevada desert, it did not tell the physicists whether it was good or bad to set off the first atomic bomb, but only that its explosion was almost certain if they fulfilled a certain number of technical conditions.

Since confusion between scientific law and moral law, between rule and norm, is very frequent among scientists, one has great difficulty in clearly distinguishing between *obligation and declaration.*

It can be very properly objected that the intellectual approach followed in this book is not so different from Bayet's. I too would like the moral concepts most useful to man to be isolated through observation and experimentation. In the last analysis I mean those moral concepts which are most conducive to happiness or stability. On this score we are in agreement. But Bayet follows an *a priori* reasoning, he excludes religions from his investigation and immediately declares their solutions antiquated. In addition his criteria "common interest," and "common conscience" are much too vague. In order to judge the correspondence of a theory to man it is better, I think, to analyze the reactions which it inspires in him in the face of suffering, sickness and death.

Let us add that when one wishes to criticize Christian morality, one should at least know it. For example Bayet writes: "if good will, good intention are the absolute good . . . why specify them with particular laws when these laws are insufficient? Why say, thou shall not kill when, everything considered, the important thing . . . is not to steal and kill except with an upright and good intention?" Now even children studying the catechism know that good intention does not absolve one from observing the natural law present, more or less clearly, in the heart of every man. A person is not responsible for an evil act performed with good intention only in the case of an *invincible ignorance,* that is to say when the person is totally ignorant of the law and had no means of knowing it. And how could a man be responsible in this case since, literally, he did not know what he was doing? Christian morality must not be confused with simple police regulations in which nobody is assumed to be ignorant of the law.

2

The Springs of Actions:
Morality and Motivation

Thus, not only are the springs of actions not purely intellectual, but neither can the study of the functions arbitrarily grouped under the name of intelligence teach us very much about what we would like to discover. We must now consider a new chapter in experimental psychology, *motivation*. It may seem difficult to give a good definition of it. Doubtlessly it will suffice for our purpose to say that it consists of a complex ensemble of instinctive dispositions, affective or intellectual according to the case and the subject, which complex governs the carrying out of a particular act.

We shall still remain faithful to the sciences and shall make the least possible use of the innumerable assertions of the philosophers. Like everything else motivation can be studied by observation and by experimentation, and in fact it has been so studied. It is not immediately apparent what motivation is in man, so we shall have to take a detour through animal psychology. For man is deeply rooted in the animal kingdom, and all experimental psychologists admit without further ado that zoopsychology constitutes the very basis of their science. Again, the more or less daring theories which were developed at the dawn of animal psychology were immediately applied to man.

Development of psychology from the acts of animals

Several decades ago, the animal organism was pictured, in short, as an inert mass which in order to act—or, better, to react—required the impact of an external stimulus. The intensity of the stimulation and the intensity of the reaction were more or less proportionate and their relations could be systematized in mathematical form. The adaptation of the organism to external environment was not denied, but it was accounted for by postulating an extremely simple mechanism of the type of the conditioned reflex. If stimulus S sets off the response R, and is habitually associated with S', at the end of a certain time, S' by itself will set off R. Conditioned reflexes may be erased, inhibited, excited and so on. There are primary and secondary conditionings. Conditioning is found at the base of learning. For example, when a rat running through a maze, enters a blind alley, the "entry-in-the-blind-alley" response is weakened little by little when the rat finds it gets no food there. On the contrary, when it finds the terminal chamber, the "entry-in-the-chamber" response is progressively reinforced, because there the rat receives a "reward in the form of food." It was imagined, therefore, that after a certain time errors would become scarce and that eventually the rat would reach the terminal chamber without making a single mistake. The phenomenon which interferes with the pattern of taking food is the theory of "need-reduction," particularly in relation to hunger. This situation is set up when the rat is deprived of food several hours before it enters the maze. Gradually, need-reduction achieved first rank among the explanatory theories of conditioning. In fact, it is a *quantity* that can be easily assessed. For example, the need to eat must be roughly proportional to the length of the period of deprivation. This likewise can be expressed mathematically, and it has been done. The great names of Pavlov and Hull will always be linked to these theories which are among the most powerful and best conceived that modern science has produced. Hull has perfected a veritable algebra of behavior, the ingenuity and rigor of which one cannot help but admire. It is important to rightly understand the mentality of the founders of the science of conditioning and learning. Before they came upon the scene, experimental psychology could barely stammer. In those days, animals suffered like us, and experienced desires and volitions. The dog had a feeling for duty, and even ants were not insensible to moral feelings(!). Then, literature abounded with tales about the mind of beasts, tales which were distinguished chiefly for their lack of judgment and abounding credulity. It was inevitable that scientists would eventually find all this irritating, above all because of the absolute impossibility of going ahead under such conditions. But going ahead toward what? Toward man? But at that time human psychology was in the hands of the philosophers to whom it would have seemed somewhat absurd to attempt to add much to the immortal analyses of Plato, Aristotle, Spinoza and the others. The *magister dixit* had begun its rule in philosophy, and one may wonder whether its triumph is not complete at the present time when philosophy is all too often reduced to historical considerations. Science could not accept a stagnant situation like that. Its aim is progress, that is to say, to exert an increasingly precise control on the world. Loeb, the "Father of Tropisms," at first interested himself in instinctive behavior and showed that if animals, such as insects, were drawn to or fled from flame, it was not at all because they feared darkness or hated light as the good Graber claimed. Rather an irresistible drive automatically draws it into the beam of light and forces the moth to hurl itself into the flame. Or else, in the contrary case, the light repels it as one magnet might repel another of like charge. In this way the study of instinctive behavior was given a physiological and mathematical bases in which *anthropomorphic extrapolation no longer played any role*. Hull and Pavlov later were to complete experimental psychology by approaching the study of learning in the same spirit.

If I dwell leisurely on considerations seemingly far removed from our purpose, it is because of the *philosophical substratum* of all these investigations. Unquestionably it was very wise to put aside as useless those speculations concerning the consciousness and feelings of animals. They cannot speak to us and will never be able to tell us anything about them. Hence, the time came when it was realized that it was not only possible, but easy and fruitful, to study animals by just observing their actions. The results that were amassed in a short time are amazing. Then, if dispensing with the consciousness worked so well, perhaps it was because consciousness was of no importance— and maybe even played no role—in *animals, and also in man*. Zoopsychologists sooner or later tend to extrapolate the results of their work in the direction of man. They are keenly aware that their studies are at the very basis of general psychology and that it is impossible for man to differ from animals absolutely and on all points. Precisely because of these continual extrapolations it is proper to give special attention to zoopsychology.

Then came the statements of men like J. B. Watson, stamped with a veritable antimetaphysical rage, "Mind is behavior, and nothing else." Consciousness is only an epiphenomenon which serves no purpose. And since it serves no purpose, it probably does not exist. With the destruction of consciousness went freedom. And very respectable researchers like Loeb confessed in all naïveté that the aim of their investigations was to prove, thanks to the irresistible character of *tropisms,* the absence of freedom. Motivation thus becomes something very simple and very elementary, a matter of "push and pull." Men and animals are subject to a small number of basic needs: hunger, thirst, sexual desire, etc., and learn to repeat an act as soon as it has been rewarded by a reduction of need. Pavlov, in a phrase which we hope was only a flash of wit, included even the need to know among conditioned responses! Obviously I am simplifying, so as to keep this exposition within proper dimensions, but the general line of the mechanist school corresponds very much to this.

Present development

Despite the shock these ideas must produce in a layman, it is important to appreciate *the extent of the service rendered to science* by these studies. The fruitfulness of these theories is undeniable: as soon as one became involved in exactly measuring phenomena that were supposedly made recognizable by giving them anthropomorphic labels, one became aware of their entirely different and much more complex natures than their labels would have suggested. For example an endless literature has been written on the white rat in the maze. It was really a stroke of genius to introduce a subject into an apparatus whose shape was constantly varied in order to measure the decrease in errors made with the progress in the training, the force of the motivation, the variations of the sensory *stimuli,* etc. Learning experiments, conducted by an attentive experimenter, give access to the domains of *1)* intelligence (through the study of the *reorganization* of the experience of the subject when the arrangement of the dead ends is altered in the course of the test), *2)* of memory (by the evaluation of the increase of errors after a more or less prolonged rest period, or of their decrease when the tests are grouped or separated in different ways), and 3) of the sensory (by noting the errors after the surgical removal of different sense organs or different parts of the brain). While the docile white rat runs around the maze, the notebooks in which the experiments are recorded fill up rapidly, because negative results are as important as the positive. American experimenters, to whom this kind of investigation is particularly agreeable, estimate there are approximately three thousand titles in the bibliography on rat learning. Obviously nobody has read all of this immense work. But some of the general lines are clear in the excellent discussions which have appeared in the books by Hilgard and Munn mentioned in the Bibliography of this book.

First cracks in the edifice of strict behaviorism

It is just such syntheses which aroused a certain disquiet among the better American researchers. First of all in the domain of sensory localization: it was observed that a blind rat could relearn the maze very rapidly by making use of tactile data; that deaf or anosmic rats could also find their way through a maze, and that a maze learned by walking was just as easily traversed by swimming, although the coordination of movements is completely different. Hence the subject possessed a pattern of sensory impressions and could without any appreciable strain transpose the directional data from one sort of action to another. Where, then, is one to place the primitive theories in which a certain zone of a specially stimulated receptor acts on a group of specific muscles and only there (Loeb)? For a while the phenomenon seemed to be based on kinesthesia, or postural sense—the instant perception of a bodily position—which appeared to offer a more supple mechanism, one more adaptable to the circumstances of the experience. Then the ingenious and philosophic Germans, who do not shrink from the most daring experiments, succeeded in transposing the learning of a mouse to a maze twice the size of the original; and again to another maze which had been altered so that what had been right angles were then acute or obtuse angles; and also to another maze which was arranged in the reflected image (as seen in a mirror) of the first. In all these cases the mouse quickly found its way. What then becomes of kinesthesia? What becomes of the sensory coordinations, even with all the transferal of impressions that one would wish?

If this were only all! *Latent learning,* however, must also be added. About twelve years ago an American investigator published a report on an amazing experiment which at first the scientific world, almost unanimously, refused to believe. He had placed a rat in a maze and let it move around at its ease, without offering it the prospect of food at a specific place; or without, as is sometimes done, giving it a vigorous electric shock when it entered a blind alley. The happy animal then ambled about the maze with a perfectly relaxed air, dawdled here and there, and it marked at random certain spots with a drop of urine. At the very same time an unhappy fellow rat labored hard in a neighboring maze, but it was subjected to the rewards and punishments of the usual experiments. Little by little, its curve of errors dropped until it could finally reach the exit with hardly an error. Now let us return to the idler in the first maze and subject him to a controlled run with rewards and punishment. *His curve of error dropped very quickly and in a short* time he overtook the control animal. Hence, in the course of its random tour the rat had fixed the image of the maze, and it had drawn, as Tolman puts it, the "cognitive map" of the maze without punishments of any kind, without anything that would permit the introduction of the old mechanist hypotheses.

Such is latent learning and one can see why the behaviorists might be discomfited in the presence of so paradoxical a phenomenon. Experimenters attacked it in all kinds of ways for many years. But now it is clear that the bases of this experiment are unshakable, and that it reveals a phenomenon even more widespread than was believed. After all how could the animal "get by" in this vast universe without some sort of a process like this? Several years ago one of my students, Henri Verron, studied learning in Blattidae (the common kitchen cockroach), at which time he told me about a series of very interesting phenomena. We were trying to detect the influence of *anisotropic* stimuli, and Verron had covered the maze with plate glass on which the subject moved freely. But immediately afterwards, when the learning was begun, not on the glass but on the actual surface of the maze, the number of errors dropped from the moment the very first runs began. Had the view of the maze through the glass been responsible for the preliminary phase? In order to make sure, Verron slipped a sheet of opaque paper under the glass and repeated the experiment. This time the first runs showed no change from the usual. The cockroach is "naïve" (in the popular American usage of that word), and when subjected to learning its number of errors is at first very high. I still think about that afternoon when Verron and I compared the number of errors and mused on the complexity of living matter, even with so primitive an animal as a cockroach. These are some of those surprises science holds in store and which reward one's efforts.

New theories of motivation

In the light of these facts we are forced to ask what remains of the classic explanation of motivation. In addition to latent learning there are other more recent experiments from America. The mischievous Professor Harlow, who flavors the severity of theoretical exposition with a dash of humor (generally directed against his colleagues) very plainly pronounced some very drastic opinions during a recent convention. He is particularly opposed to the theory of drive–reduction. Professor Harlow gave some monkeys a little mechanical problem, to open a bolt locked by several pins which had to be removed in a certain order. The rhesus monkeys on which the experiment was conducted have enormous jowls where they store food. Harlow permitted them to gorge themselves before the experiment and they did not fail to do so. Soon their jowls were stuffed with hazelnuts and raisins which they could grab at will. It was then that they were set before the bolt which was to be opened. First observation: it interested them very much. Then they put a little food in their jowls as they turned the device around their agile fingers. If the bolt resisted, the monkey let it go for awhile and reached for another raisin or hazelnut as if to give himself encouragement. Finally they solved the problem. A second important observation: the monkey never gave up. On the contrary he fiddled with the pins and bolts as if he were trying to fix it, and this lasted a long time. On the other hand a hungry rhesus attacked the problem in a hasty manner, seemed incapable of proceeding with the necessary calm, and gave it up as soon as he found the solution. Can it be that these powerful drives of hunger or thirst, the very motors of learning, have no role at all in the learning process or at most a disrupting one? This idea immediately put Harlow in a capricious mood and he suggested modestly that the Lord had undoubtedly overlooked the "drive-reduction theory" when he created the rhesus and allowed his evolution. The langur monkeys of India also learn easily, despite a stomach with multiple pockets which allows them to store up food for very long periods of time.

Meyer worked anew on the hungry rhesus, not fed for 2 to 22 hours, according to the case, without noting any differences in the performances during the course of discrimination problems. Birch came to the same conclusion working with young chimpanzees; and Strassburger, Sheffield and Rory, with the rat. Old experiments were dug up which reported the good results of a distribution of food *before* and not *after* the learning. And these facts compelled the S-R theorists to indulge in some of those intellectual acrobatics at which they are past masters.

A hedonic process of motivation

Young already finds it very complicated to evaluate the behavior of a rat before sugar solutions of different concentrations. For example: if a normally fed animal is permitted access to an inclosure containing a bowl of sugared water, the rat's run toward the water will be the faster the more concentrated the solution. The time of latency, that is to say the rat's delay before going through the door that is opened for it, is shorter the longer the subject has been left in contact with the solution. No drive-reduction can explain such behavior.

Young believes that such behavior stems neither from stimuli nor from responses; but from *central processes,* and the American writer thinks this is proved by his experiments with sodium chloride. Richter had already shown that rats without adrenal glands have a great need of salt and recognize it much more readily than normal rats, even in very weak concentrations. But he thought that the whole problem of discrimination and its variations was more or less secondary and was actually the result of a modification of the sensitivity of the sense organs. But along came Pfaffman and Bare who measured the nervous discharge in the nerve of the tongue of rats without adrenal glands who were given a salt solution to drink. What happened? The discharge was the same as in normal rats! But if the subjects are simultaneously offered a series of bowls containing different concentrations of sodium chloride, they can differentiate much weaker solutions of salt water from pure water than can normal rats. Hence it is the *threshold of preference* and not the sensory threshold which is decisive. The process is central—it implies higher nerve *centers,* and it is decidedly not simple.

This reverses everything we thought we knew about the conditions of a good experiment and in particular about the naïve idea that the more an animal is fond of a food or drink, the more he will eat or drink it. This is true only under particular conditions which are set up in the experiment. When sugar solutions are *permanently* available, the 9 per cent concentration is preferred almost constantly. But if the preference test is brief, the strongest solution is preferred exclusively, even if it is a thick syrup. The analogy to human behavior under the same conditions is glaring. A preference can be changed therefore, by surfeiting the subject with his favorite food: thus habits are established according to needs. But once established, the habit tends to continue regardless of need. This is to say that we must speak of pleasure and pain even in connection with a rat who drinks sugared water. If this seems completely obvious to the layman, the conclusion nevertheless remains a most astonishing one for the scientist.

Butler's experiment

A mischievous genie must have prompted Harlow to undertake this experiment which he performed with his student, Butler, the results of which allowed him once more to twit Hull's disciples, those S-R theorists whom he simply cannot bear. Butler encircled the cage of a monkey with a box with opaque walls and subjected the animal, well taken care of in other respects, to a simple discrimination test: to distinguish between two cards bearing different designs. When the positive card was shown and chosen, a little window opened and the animal, as a reward, was permitted to look outside to satisfy its curiosity (however much one may try to maintain an objective language which simply states facts, how the devil can this be expressed otherwise?). The most remarkable thing is that all went well and the monkey succeeded in his visual discrimination without firing a shot, so to speak. How can this phenomenon be interpreted if need-reduction is the only drive for learning?

Brown, a disciple of Hull, tried hard to extricate himself from this fix. One of his arguments is worth its weight in gold and I cannot resist the pleasure of citing it. It is true, he admits, that the deprivation of food for eight hours does not yield any better results than those obtained after only an hour of abstinence, but after all these results are not worse! Then, stung by Harlow's taunts, he tries to frighten him by pointing out where Butler and his monkey will lead him if he does not watch out: if the monkey can look out the window, this satisfies his "curiosity-drive" so well "that responses followed by an increase in drive tend to be learned" which, oh sacrilege!, is the very opposite of that asserted by the theorists of drive-reduction. Since Harlow apparently did not fear such excommunication, Brown lost himself in considerations that are too nebulous for me to linger over.

Conclusion

What's the point one may ask, of this long dissertation on the modern aspects of animal psychology in a book devoted to the God of the scientists? The dissertation is essentially intended to *dispel prejudice*. And since one cannot refrain from comparing animal and man, it is better to start from an adequate conception of the former. Now, what do we see at the present time? The classic mechanistic conceptions now seem ridiculously simple to us. Despite their past usefulness, they have had their day, and we must rid ourselves of them. There is no such thing as a simple stimulus, an isolated response; these are manufactures of the laboratory. Pavlov's dog was not only conditioned by the sound of the bell, but also by the white coat of the operator, the general appearance of the place, and still many other things. If we give it a lump of sugar as a reward, the consequences will be complex, according to the state of the animal, at what moment we give it the sugar, and the general setup of the experiment. This single response to an agreeable stimulus involves not only a receptor, a *nerve chain* and a muscle, but the whole of the organism under the aegis of the central nervous system—that is to say the highest mechanisms of behavior.

Now the organism itself appears to us in an entirely new light. This has been clearly seen by a school of "objectivist" psychologists, partisans of "outdoor" observation as opposed to the rigid methods of the laboratory. According to this school the animated machine is not a "lazy ass" (to use von Holst's term) which waits for the whip of the stimulus before it moves; it is a spirited horse always trying to go. But only the object of a future action (the female if the need for copulation predominates or food, if it is hunger), and it alone will be able to lower the barrier which prevents the thoroughbred from flinging itself outside. When no object presents itself "the electricity accumulates" and the discharge of activity will even take place "in a vacuum." The objectivist theories contain a throng of exciting and revolutionary considerations but this is not the place to develop them.

Nevertheless, one particular point which was not lost on the objectivists merits special attention: this is *exploratory activity*. In fact when the organism has nothing specific to do, when it has received its ration of sleep, food and sexual satisfaction, it does not stop because of this *but it explores,* without respite, in some way just for the pleasure of it. Like the hunting dog who looks for game although he feels no hunger, the organism moves about in the vast universe with the aid of its legs or sight, and it collects impressions. This is an absolutely universal behavior which we have observed in connection with latent learning and with Butler's monkey. My pupil Darchen found this behavior, and studied it in the greatest detail in the Blattidae (kitchen cockroach). Here perhaps is the key, or one of the keys, which would give us access to an understanding of the organism. Is this not just what the layman discerns when he exclaims, "It moves . . . it's alive!" Just imagine what all this activity implies, concerning which one must not develop a too narrowly mechanical schema, *this pursuit of the collection of images with no other aim than this collecting* itself! If along with the old psychologists we admit that the animal is moved by his "instincts," here indeed is one of the most powerful and most widespread . . .

It is becoming difficult to separate radically exploratory activity and man's need to know; this need so well suggested by the monkey in the course of manipulating his pegged bolt "gratuitously." Here then is a complete reversal of the situation in psychology. The old system begins by making as simple a diagram as possible of the animal as the facts seem to warrant, with physical analogies borrowed from the lever, the wheelbarrow, and from the most rudimentary machines. Starting out thus, since man is an animal, one discovers in him (or believes that one will discover) the same gross affects, the same combinations of tropic stimuli, needs and reflexes that are being reduced to mathematical terms in the animal. Evidently, in such a perspective, freedom, consciousness, and mind, quickly find themselves in a poor position.

But under the pressure of facts, and in some way from within itself (this is certainly the most important), the system is forced to modify itself. This is not because the experiments on which it rested were false. But it must be granted that they were all of the same type, that the unconscious of the experimenter chose them, without positively willing it in such a way that they tend to prove his point. For example, an animal locked up in a cage, not having eaten for a long time and confronted with a problem about which it can understand nothing, will solve it by chance and will acquire the habit of movements without meaning, simply because these actions bring a morsel of the coveted food. So the animal is judged stupid, automatized, subject to simple and blind reflexes. Of course! As Harlow says, it then resembles a subject without a cerebral cortex, without that organ capable of the greatest psychic accomplishments. But let us modify the conditions, let the animals function, without bothering them, after having fed them normally, and without administering either punishment or immediate rewards. Then completely different results emerge which disclose the other aspect of the organism to us. And it is a *humanized* aspect (all proportions duly considered), whereas the mechanist theories present us a *bestialized* image of *man*. Here we can recognize the roots of our tendencies, of our curiosity, and perhaps of our need to know. Certain experiments, like latent learning and the sudden solution of a problem after reflection (with the monkey), inevitably imply a consciousness, no matter how rudimentary (but not necessarily, as with man, consciousness to the second degree, *the consciousness of consciousness*).

The doors of the mechanist prison have been thrown open, but let us not delude ourselves: consciousness, mind, and freedom unquestionably will emerge very much changed after this plunge into the depths and it is not certain that scientists will accommodate themselves for very long to conceptions borrowed from Greek philosophers and formulated in a language too different from theirs. It will be necessary to make many reinterpretations.

In the light of these new theories one can better understand the propositions set forth by Koehler and Lorenz. Heretofore, investigators have tried to study behavior in its very first beginnings, among the simplest and lowest animals. But nothing is more obscure than a beginning (Koehler). Would it not be possible to consider man as the end product and supreme ornament of psychic evolution, and *to start with him*, moving down the scale to the animal and finding in it more clearly the adumbration of his own tendencies, feelings, and ways of acting? Would not a new anthropomorphism, free of the naïve interpretations of yore, constitute a profitable tactic for explorers of nature?

Human motivation

Obviously our inquiry on motivation will take us to man. But a serious disappointment awaits us, because here experiments and measurements are infinitely less extensive than with animals. First of all this results from the particular difficulty of the material, and also perhaps from inhibitions brought about by certain theories. This tendency of considering only the most simple phenomena as comprehensible has led, as Harlow says, to the more and more careful *study of less and less interesting phenomena!* I shall not have much to say on the question of how a man decides or does not decide to do this or that, except for some details that do not touch upon the fundamental core of the problem.

The difficulties

Our needs, tendencies and judgments are inextricably mixed. The man who pretends to judge from the view point of Sirius is quite often only naïve, ignorant, and a bad psychologist. It is curious to see science turn away from the impassive Minerva and explode (in the course of examining the concrete) the well-entrenched categories which the goddess Reason of the eighteenth and nineteenth centuries had tried to transform into impregnable fortresses.

Let us first examine some unexpected factors which enter into the formation of a judgment. We shall be able to do this only in a very fragmentary way. It is not a question of outlining a complete picture of the studies on human motivation that have been made up to the present time, but only: *1)* of citing some examples thereof which will show the complexity of the problem; *2)* of illustrating the role of the great metaphysical questions on this motivation by citing some modern observations, even though too brief.

Some unexpected factors in the formation of opinions and perception

Man acts, more or less, according to his opinions or those which he thinks he has. But man's profoundly social character must not be forgotten, and all modern investigations stress this peculiarity. Man does not form ideas or lines of conduct in the abstract or in isolation, but by reference to his social group with which he is continually exchanging stimuli. *But not in a simple way.* Let us recall here Fritz Heider's rule of cognitive harmony: The equilibrium is unstable when an act with a positive force field is attributed to a person whose force field is negative or vice-versa. The disharmony can then be solved in three ways: the valence sign of the act is changed in order to make it agree with the sign of the person accomplishing the act; or else the sign of the actor is changed; or finally there is a cognitive and, we shall add a *motivational* divorce perhaps between the act and the actor. Finally the group is able to tolerate disharmony in a more or less prolonged and more or less conscious way.

The extent of eventual change of an opinion evidently depends on the extent of credibility accorded to new information which goes against it. Hovland and Weiss carried out an amusing experiment with American students by showing them magazine articles taken (allegedly) from *Fortune* or *Pravda*. It was noted, as one might expect that the young Americans did not believe what they read in the *Pravda* articles. But in measuring the *persistence of opinion* (over the course of time) a new phenomenon appeared which is difficult to explain. After four weeks the number of opinions which agreed with the source accorded high credibility (*Fortune*) diminished, and an increase in the percentage of those trusting the source of low credibility (*Pravda*) was observed. *Resistance to the acceptance of an assertion one at first opposes diminishes with time.* This is a little fact which makes us aware of our ignorance in a matter where more precise data would be of such great consequence. Let us add that Keller and Volkart obtained completely similar results (changing with time) by having boy scouts listen to a lecture against camping.

Festinger has further extended the study of changes in opinion in relation to the structure of the group. At first he proposed a discussion of no great importance to the group (a football play), then another on which agreement is more difficult (what to do with delinquent children?). At the same time the group was subjected to three types of pressure, high, average, and low. In the first case they were told that they *must* come to agreement, in the second they were warned that there is a correct answer and they would be given a certain number of points according to whether or not they came close to it. In the third case they were advised that they had only to discuss the problem. One immediately observes, as was reasonable to expect, that the opinions tended the more to uniformity the higher the pressure. The experimenter declared to one of the groups that it was intentionally composed of very different individuals; and to another group, on the contrary, that it was composed of subjects completely like each other. After this the tendency to uniformity was less great in the group called heterogeneous than in the homogeneous group. This was particularly noticeable with the football problem—the resistance to change was already very strong in the matter of delinquent children. Above all, however, *the groups had a tendency to exclude extreme individuals from the discussion* and to formulate a homogeneous and average opinion for themselves.

At first sight it is not easy to reconcile these experiments by Festinger with the work of Thouless on the *tendency to certainty in religious beliefs*. When certain very lively discussions in a group clearly arrange themselves for or against a belief in the religious order, then the result is not the adoption by the majority of a certain degree of conviction, but the "secretion" of two types of diametrically opposed convictions. After analyzing numerous questionnaires, Thouless believed he could assert that "beliefs" are deeply held for or against, while "scientific assertions" are much more finely naunced. This is because the former have to do not with the domain of pure thought, but that of action. Scepticism, or even the suspension of judgment, seem nonhabitual or unstable, contrary to what one might think.

From this too succinct and fragmentary data, therefore, one may conclude that the subtle influence of the group acts in many different directions, but it acts with violence in the religious domain (motivational).

The influence of the temperament and personality

As many authors have suggested, religious beliefs—or as I prefer to say, psychic motivational dispositions—perhaps depend on the constitution or the personality. Here we are forced to enter the domain of characterology which it is not completely impossible for a scientist to do. But he must at least have the courage to break through the innumerable dams of paper, uselessly printed, heaped up by authors of a purely literary training who are nevertheless fascinated by the problems of personality and character. Of late, certain American studies based on the use of the questionnaire and the opinionnaire tend to delimit the scientific frontiers of the science of characterology.

But we must not hide the fact that here we are as pioneers armed only with poorly refined techniques particularly difficult to use. Nevertheless let us see what has been produced in the sector which interests us.

In 1952 Dreger applied a combination of tests to a vast series of subjects and believed that as a conclusion he could reject a series of hypotheses: first, the hypothesis that subjects holding liberal opinions in religion manifest a greater emotional maturity than conservatives, the "integrists." It is likewise false that there is a correlation between the rigidity of mental structure and a "conservative" religious attitude. All the emotional types are randomly distributed among "liberals" and "conservatives" in matters of religion. It is false to assert that conservatives are guided more by the feeling of sin, and the liberals more by reason. Finally, one can no longer say that conservatives dwell less than do liberals on controversial religious situations which usually provoke their reactions of aggressiveness. At best it must be admitted that the "dependence need" is clearer among the conservatives than the liberals. Thouless finds no correlation at all between belief and nonbelief and the degree of intelligence.

It must be concluded that up to now efforts to link the religious mind (or of the attitudes within this mind) to a simple factor have failed. The fact is that religion unquestionably impregnates very deep beds which are externally manifested in a polymorphic manner.

Variations with age

Will we find more information on the evolution of beliefs as the development of the individual proceeds? I am afraid that even here the investigations are not sufficiently advanced to guide us in any sure manner. Nelson questioned 300 students, 14 years after graduation from the college where they had first been studied: 35 per cent viewed religion with more favor than formerly, 38 per cent felt that their conviction of the existence of God had increased, and 24 per cent felt it had diminished. *Largely the attitudes had remained very stable* and had resisted the multiple shocks of existence. Nevertheless, on the whole the attitudes evolved toward a greater rigidity in the consideration of religious problems, except in those areas in which serious socio-economic questions were raised. Here the development toward liberalism was emphatic.

Attitudes in the face of fundamental problems

I thought to arrive more easily at the deep strata of motivation with an analysis of the *attitudes in face of death*. It seemed to me that the bases of the personality should then reveal themselves more easily.

But there is nothing of this sort at all, or else experimental psychology is not sufficiently advanced to tell us anything on this score. And even that which it can tell us seems very disconcerting. Stacey and Reichen (1954) studying a series of 15-year-old girls, normal and retarded (the intelligence quotient of the latter was barely over 65) found that the retarded girls were more affected by the idea of death than the normal ones, but they thought about death less often. They more often declared that they would change their way of life completely if they were sure of a future life. But, as a matter of fact, relatively few of the girls in both groups ever thought about death often, or wished to die. Middleton worked on 400 college students and found that 92 per cent thought only very rarely about death, and only during a crisis of depression, bad luck, or the death of a near relative. About 50 per cent deliberately avoided funeral services and 20 per cent experienced a lasting depression after attending a burial ceremony. But 43 per cent liked to read poems about death, "this did not do anything to them," or they even found a certain solace in the reading. It must be noted that 62 per cent were practically indifferent to the thought of death and that only 12 per cent held it in horror; 68 per cent believed in the future life, but 64 per cent declared that if they were sure it existed, they would in no wise change their manner of life, 25 per cent would introduce some changes and 9 per cent a radical change.

Hence the thought of death practically does not enter into everyday motivations, save among a very small number of individuals. Moreover it is not viewed in a very realistic manner. As Bergson has already observed, "homo sapiens" mainly defends himself against motivational poisons by not thinking about them.

As was to be expected, this indifference is particularly clear among children. Schilder and Wechsler (1934) noted that before a corpse children were especially struck by the fact that "it" did not "move any more." But the child does not draw any conclusion about his own death and does not believe in a complete stop, strictly irreversible. The flow of time in particular is in no way linked to the idea of death. But the child willingly thinks about the death of others, above all about violent death. Death does not appear to him as the natural end of life, but is linked to the idea of the hostility of others or of punishment.

General conclusions on human motivation

These conclusions will be very disappointing. In the light of the recent works of zoopsychologists, it seems scientifically probable that the animal is not a *simple* and crude machine obeying only well-specified *stimuli*. Its desire for exploration is much more lively than that desire of animals which already constitutes the basis of behavior. Hence we are a far cry from the animal-machine and consequently from the man-machine, so dear to lingering materialists. For if there is a machine, it is of a completely different type and much more complex than those we manufacture.

But *we scarcely know what makes it go*. Multiple influences, unconscious for the most part, regulate behavior, and the composition of the social group is one of the most powerful of these influences. However, the attitude toward religious problems does not stand in any clear correlation with any well-determined character trait. The fundamental options are not chosen and the attitude generally remains passive. Man lets himself be guided more than he guides himself, without posing questions to himself. When questions do come up, for example in connection with a future life, he has no idea of a relation between the solution he adopts and his behavior.

One can think of several causes for these amorphous results:

1) The possible inadequacy of the questionnaires and tests. This, I think, is a very probable hypothesis: it involves questions that are too complex for the subjects to answer easily.

2) Few men, moreover, are *conscious of the motives* which make them act and it would be very difficult to devise an "opinionnaire" on the matter.

3) Finally the Bergsonian observation is still valid, as I quoted it previously: the species avoids the problems which would prevent it from acting.

A "positive theology," as well as a positive morality, still remain to be established. What does man think of God, and why does he act in a specific manner? Experimental psychology cannot yet answer these questions.

Let us therefore turn to another discipline, the history of religion. For certain men among the human species do not refuse to let their brain function, even in the presence of anxiety. They continue to explore, they "secrete" religions. . . . What do they teach us about the "chemistry of the act?"

3

Man Seeks for a Reason to Live Throughout the History of Religions

If it is ridiculous to attempt in a few pages a synthesis of the history of religions—which is, moreover, outside my field of competence—nevertheless it seems indispensable to have some idea of the awakening and the development of theotropic activity. And since religious ideas and notions give body to a great part of behavior, I must, out of faithfulness to my purpose, sort out their influence on motivation.

Prehistory

Of course the absence of written documents in prehistory is cruelly felt. But man has left numerous traces of his history and a zoopsychologist knows very well that the acts of individuals introduce us very deeply into their psyche.

First, the custom of *burial* with funeral offerings (weapons, food remnants) is of incredible antiquity. At Moustier, for example, the dead person keeps a beautiful stone hatchet near at hand. The skulls are often arranged by themselves in cavities. But the most curious thing is the use of *red ocher*, present in all the first burial places. Often, the corpse is laid out on a bed of ocher with which his bones have been rubbed. Among many present-day noncivilized peoples, all kinds of medico-magical virtues are still attributed to red ocher: it helps to cauterize wounds, retards decomposition to a certain extent, and so on. On the other hand it has the color of blood which makes it a symbol of life. In the light of what we now know about its use, it seems probable that primitive peoples utilized it in order to preserve or reanimate the vital energies of the dead person.

Among *primitive peoples* of the present day, burial with offerings still means *belief in survival.* I don't think that there are any exceptions. Therefore we can infer that the belief was already in existence even several hundreds of thousands of years before our era. There are many other traces of a very ancient religious cult (the Altar of the Bear, for example), but we know practically nothing about it. Again I repeat that my aim is of course, not to embrace the history of religions as a whole, but only to stick to those driving ideas that are important for motivation, and to neglect the details of their ceremonies.

Burial places become more complicated from the neolithic period on. Sometimes the tomb is surmounted by megaliths. Around the dead are placed musical instruments, drums and bull-roarers. Now in all actual primitive civilizations these utensils either drive away, or call forth, spirits. Belief in survival appears more and more evident: it is, moreover, the only data of a religious nature about which we are completely sure. Thus, man must have discovered, practically from the time of his origin, a means to palliate the idea of death, which, as Bergson might say, is an obstacle to the will to live.

Present-day primitive peoples are as old as we are, and their religious thought has had time to become diversified. However, it is still exciting to study this thought, because primitive peoples have more of an opportunity to be close to the origins, *thanks to their tendency to "sclerosis"* . . . The lightning-like evolutions through which the Western white man has passed seem to be totally unknown among them—unless these are unleashed under the white man's influence. Their main preoccupation is to repeat what their fathers have done or, better still, to imitate the acts of a mythical ancestor point by point. The best example of this is the frightful obsession of the Dogons of Bandiagara, whom Griaule finds full of genius. I wonder why. Perhaps they have preserved better than we have the image of origins, when the springs of the human soul functioned naïvely and showed themselves in their nakedness.

The studies of the great historian, Mircea Eliade, are of capital importance for the understanding of these basic springs. For the time is past when some very simple theories could pretend to enlighten us about the primitive mentality, with its prelogical character. As a matter of fact, Lévy-Bruhl, who had created the notion of the pre-logical mentality, did not believe in it very much himself toward the end of his life and was disposed to admit the existence of numerous "prelogics" among us civilized moderns. Also, what are we to say about the diffused power (*mana, wakan, orenda,* etc.) which impreg-nated so many objects and notions, if we believe overhasty ethnolo-gists? Have there not been at least twenty different attempts, hastily made, to account for the origin of religions, now as stemming from magic alone, now from the cult of the dead alone, and so on? We are today much less hurried and less ambitious. With the aid of concrete examples we must content ourselves with tracing the variations of an idea through different civilizations without forgetting that if analogy is the most useful of reasoning procedures, it is also the most dangerous. As Gabriel Marcel would say, "When two men do the same thing, it is not the same thing." If we fail to take this into consideration, we will build only edifices à la Frazer, the beauty of which equals their fragility.

The hierophanies

Eliade often uses the technical terms "hierophany" and "kratophany" to characterize the manifestations of power or of the sacred. Some-times the hierophanies are difficult to interpret, like the May-pole of the countrysides. Sometimes, on the contrary, as in that widespread theme of the Cosmic Tree, the underlying symbolism easily emerges. But hierophanies imply the same meaning, the same idea, that of the rhythmic regeneration of life and of vegetation. It does not matter whether the idea is found clearly or not in the consciousness of men. Likewise all sympathetic magic and all practices of witchcraft pre-suppose a space-web connecting very distant objects with the help of a physiological sympathy directed by specific laws. Even if the witch doctor does not know this space-web in an explicit manner, he implies it in his practices.

Civilized man recoils in fear and even disgust from the idea of sacred stones and waters and from the sacredness which can suffuse the oddest objects. But Eliade proposes an interpretation as daring as it is interesting: the very variety of these hierophanies strongly expresses the idea that *the divine can incarnate itself*, thanks to its infinite freedom and power. The most humble fetishes become prefigures of the incarnation of Christ. According to Vaishnavism, Eliade recalls, Vishnu in his love for mankind shows himself in avatars (the holy basil, the salagrama stones) according to the proper modality of being peculiar to them. And this attests to his freedom to assume any form whatsoever. The theologians of the Middle Ages had already observed that God is not limited in his possibilities of incarnation, and could manifest himself if need be in a stone or an animal. Now, according to Eliade—and I strongly share his view—even though the villagers who adore the avatars do not go searching as far as the subtle *Vaishnava* theoretician, *what they do means practically the same thing*. Likewise, for the primitive man, various physiological acts, sexuality, nutrition (and even defecation among the Australian aborigenes) are *ceremonies* through which he seeks to communicate with the vital force. However, he cannot truly achieve this communication except by very exactly repeating the acts of the archetype, of the mythical ancestor.

Let us point out in passing, since we are speaking of vital force, that the notion of *mana* is neither universal nor isolated and is often accompanied by other ideas, like that of the Great Inactive God (to be discussed later): it is not *the* manifestation, it is *one of the* manifestations of the sacred. Radin, moreover, observes that with the Sioux and Algonquians *wakan* and *manito* (which have been compared to *mana*) also have the meaning of strong, strange, important, wondrous, but without implying the idea of necessarily inherent power.

In a general manner, if it is quite true that the great natural spectacles have conjured up specifically religious ideas; the phenomenon, as we shall see, is much more complicated than was imagined formerly. It was believed, for example, that thunder begot fear, and that fear begot the idea of a superior power. It is completely otherwise.

The sky and the Great Inactive God

Universal belief in a divine, celestial being, creator of the universe, who in granting rain is the guarantor of the fecundity of the earth, is now well proven. This is chiefly due to the investigations which accompanied and followed the celebrated work of Father Wilhelm Schmidt[1] and the establishment of the review *Anthropos*. Certain criticisms that have been made in connection with this matter, like Leenhardt's, do not detract from the convincing character of the work. These criticisms chiefly claim that the mind of primitive peoples cannot sustain the idea of unity. For them everything is expressed in pairs (the myths of Papa and Rangi in Polynesia, of Uranus and Gaea). Perhaps the primitive mind cannot *sustain* the idea of unity, but observation teaches us that it can *form* it. It is true that the Great God is almost immediately thrown back into a certain inactivity, but this inactivity is not quite total and the Supreme Being is invoked in solemn moments, for example, when the tribe is in danger. It is also true that all primitive peoples unanimously assert that he formerly lived among men, but *that he has withdrawn from them.*

The Supreme Being is endowed with prescience and an infinite wisdom. The moral laws and the rituals (especially the initiation rite) were introduced by him during the course of his brief sojourn on earth. He watches over the observance of his laws. He is good and wishes no evil to men: this is why savages, essentially practical, concern themselves more with evil spirits than with him. He is often called "father." The most characteristic denomination perhaps remains that of *Zeus-Dyaus* (from the root *div*—"to shine") which did not take long to become *Dyaus-pitr* (Jupiter) God-father. Among the Australians of the east coast, the women and children do not know the name of the great God Daramulun, which is reserved to the initiates, and call him papang (father) or biamban (master).

Where do the primitives get the idea of the Supreme God? Very

---

[1] *Ursprung des Gottesidee*, 12 vols. Münster in Westphalia: Aschendorff, 1912-1955.

probably from the contemplation of the vault of heaven. For no matter how effaced they may become in spots, the images of the great God always preserve a link with Uranian and meteoric phenomena. The essential weapon of the great God is thunder or lightning. When a thunderstorm rages, the Semang cut themselves with a piece of bamboo and throw the blood *toward the sky* in order to appease the Supreme Being. It apparently is, moreover, the only worship which they render him. Lightning flashes are also Yahweh's arrows, and *Dyaus* is the brilliant sky. However, "one cannot reduce the great God to his Uranian kratophany." As Eliade says, "Though the symbolism and religious values of the sky are not deduced logically from a calm and objective observation of the heavens, neither are they exclusively the product of mythical activity and nonrational religious experience. . . . Even before any religious values have been set upon the sky it reveals its transcendence. The sky 'symbolizes' transcendence, power and changelessness simply by being there. It exists because it is high, infinite, immovable, powerful."[2] This brings us back to an idea defended on several occasions in this book: namely that we must be wary of overstrict categories. There is not, and there never was, a question of a reasoning reason on the one side, and mythical fable-making on the other. They are joined by inextricable links. A natural phenomena gave "the idea of something" to primitive man, and what he concludes therefrom is not the one and only image of the phenomenon, nor a purely "intellectual" notion. I shall return to this point later on in the chapter.

Moreover, with the hypothesis of the exclusive role of the vault of heaven how is one to explain the other characteristics of the Great God? If he is powerful, why is he good, father, creator, and guardian of the laws which he has given? And above all what does this strange *myth of departure* mean: why did he live among men and later withdraw himself from them?

Let us rapidly review the other perhaps less important hierophanies: The solar hierophanies tend to become the privilege of an aristocracy, in contrast to other hierophanies. Very often sun worship blends with the worship of the sovereign, a phenomenon particularly

[2]*Patterns in Comparative Religion.* Translated by Rosemary Sheed (New York and London, 1958), p. 39.

developed in ancient Egypt. The sun speaks to man of might, of a unique power . . .

But *the moon* speaks to him of universal rhythm, to which the ideas of periodic resurrection (the phases of the moon), of the newly regenerated man, and of initiatory death as prelude to a new life, inevitably associated themselves with the lunar cults. And it also speaks to him of the flight of time (the moon serves to measure it), of destiny, and of the contraries of good and evil (the darkness of a moonless night). Becoming, with the idea of eternal recurrence, is perhaps the dominant idea.

The accounts of origins are linked to *the waters*, the belief that man is born of water, the idea of deluge, of second death, and of the initiatory death that we see reappear under another form. But above all "the immersion means a temporary reintegration into the formless" (Eliade) which is followed by a new creation. The waters purify and regenerate (the feeling of having been lightened after a bath).

The stone strikes the mind by its solidity, its duration, its size, and its majesty. If it stands upright it often indicates a center of the world, an omphalos. The stone is a sign of place; it was only secondarily that upright stones were to receive a phallic signification.

The earth is the universal mother, because it limitlessly brings forth new fruits. "It is the universal matrix in which one buries the dead in order that they may be regenerated." The comparison of the earth to woman is inevitable. We shall find it in the agrarian hierophanies.

Vegetation speaks of unlimited abundance; again, and always, of regeneration, of periodic rebirth. The vegetal hierophanies are so numerous that a volume would not exhaust them. To them must be linked the widely spread notion of the Cosmic Tree, the mythical giant tree that joins heaven and hell. Many gods nest in its branches; heroes and *shamans* scale it in order to arrive at wisdom. The ash tree Yggdrasil does not belong to the Teutonic religion only: it is simply a particular instance.

Agriculture is linked to the *orgy*. Just as the seeds break up underground and become something else so do men dissolve themselves in the orgy, experiencing the chaotic primordial state anew and drawing therefrom new forces, in order to be born to a new life on the morrow.

But agriculture also teaches man about the analogy between woman and field, between generative act and sowing, about death understood as a regression and, of course, the possibility of a resurrection like the seed. If the seed does not die, it cannot revive.

Numerous heirophanies are linked to the ideas of *temple*, of *palace*, of the *center of the world*, and consecrated area, into which it is at once dangerous and desirable to enter. Each house, in a certain way, can coincide with the center of the world because its main pillar will mark the axis, or again will blend with the tree of life. For the *shaman* it suffices that he climb the main pillar of the *Yurt*[3] to assimilate the Cosmic Tree and to reach the sky. Eliade notes that the desire to find oneself in sacred space corresponds to the desire to return to the sacred time, to the primordial times of the origins, to eternity. Perhaps this desire blends with the desire for stability? Does not man wish to become, as we read in the *Book of the Dead*, "the Stable One, son of the Stable One, born in the Land of Stability"? He will arrive there once again by repeating the acts of the archetype, of the sacred ancestor, by becoming this ancestor himself. And only this gives value to everyday actions and fits them into the real world.

In order to complete this extremely schematic picture of religious responses, let us add one particularity which concerns the priest, the medicine man, the *shaman*: this is the *unremitting search for ecstasy*. Primitive man seems completely convinced of the existence of a gate opening upon the other world. But access is permitted only to rare privileged persons, expert in magico-religious practice. In order to bring on ecstasy, they often go through atrocious sufferings of initiations and through prolonged privations. They swallow different poisons, because long before William James they suspected the kinship between drunkenness, other forms of intoxication, and mystical states. And, sometimes, success crowned their efforts. Then, they would declare, "we saw the light, we found the light, we became immortals." Let us with Eliade add that it is a complete exaggeration to confuse all *shamans* with common psychopaths. If it is true that particular nervous dispositions favor the vocation of *shaman*, and that in all primitive societies mentally ill persons are considered to be

---

[3] A hut used by Laplanders and Sayonedes [Trans. note].

closer to the divine, the state of being a *shaman* certainly requires other capacities which are not at all the accomplishments associated with psychopaths. It seems that in many tribes the *shaman* must possess a perfect self-control, he must be agile, robust, intelligent and often very wily. And he must have learned the host of traditions of his people; which are often so complicated that one can hardly see how a neurotic could assimilate them all. Certain Eskimo *shamans* can recite traditional poems for *several days* in a row without exhausting their store.

Let us summarize here: In general primitive man believes in a Great God who is separated from men because of their own fault. He is good, and is invoked only in exceptional circumstances. He has neither a cult nor an image. There exists another world to which the dead go: no one knows what it is really like, but it is something dark, dangerous and frightening. Faults are punished on this earth by the Great God or by other gods, but they are often material faults in which the intention barely plays a role. There exists, however, a natural morality but it only applies within the clan. There is also another world, most often outside the abode of the dead: it is the sacred world where the ancestors dwell, in which time and space are not the same as here below, and to which one gains access through ecstasy. Sacred time and space establish contacts with the terrestrial world, and it is very important to know about them in order to utilize them.

One can be regenerated, one can live again, "having been reduced to zero" on this earth. This is permitted by initiation techniques and periodic rites. Then life is prolonged, health returns, and evil influences are exorcised.

Consequently motivation is purely earthly. It is on this earth that one seeks advantages; it is on this earth that an alliance must be made with the gods so that they will accord you life, health, fortune, sexual potency, success in the hunt, and an abundant harvest. Man has already exorcised death (but only partially), as the Bergsonian theory claims, because it does not swoop down by chance: it is rather a punishment of the Gods, or a vengeance. Hence it can be avoided by assuring oneself of the friendship of the Powers who rule the world.

Yet in this very material picture there is a burgeoning of confused notions which later are to undergo a magnificent development: the idea of the Other World, the Opposite Pole of the World, of a good and Sovereign Power toward which the soul of the person in ecstasy sometimes takes wing . . .

The great religions

The great religions exhibit these two currents, the temporal and the spiritual, one alternately dominating the other through the centuries. Often, the beginnings are basely temporal. Piety toward the gods assures happiness on this earth; the other life inspires only sadness and terror. Consequently, sometimes, after several centuries, religious reformers, or else the deep needs of the human soul, direct further attention to the other world. Little by little the motivation changes so that in the end it tends rapidly toward the mysteries and the rituals which procure happiness and immortality in the future world: it is the old idea of regeneration which finds its full flowering here. At the same time piety ceases to be only a business deal, or the strict carrying out of rites compelling, so to speak, the divinity to fulfill the wishes of the suppliant. Piety becomes more tender: "Bhakti," as the Hindus call it, develops, and one does good because it is pleasing to God. But in many cases the phenomena are far from unfolding in accordance with so regulated an order, and it happens that the spiritualist current can reveal itself from the beginning at the same time as the materialist current. Now, while "materialist" religions are often the oldest and the first to appear, *it is not always this way*. Very ancient Egyptian beliefs already show the most lively interest in the other world and a lofty conception of morality and divinity.

The materialist religions

These correspond very well to static religion as described by Bergson. Unquestionably the most ancient are the *Asian religions* (Sumerian, Akkadian, ancient Canaanite and Semitic religions). They correspond to cults that were essentially naturist, very close to primitive ideas on fecundity, the return of the seasons, and the alternation of light and darkness. The gods are poorly individualized, very numerous, and sacrifices are made to them to appease their anger after a fault has been committed. But there is no official "credo." There is no question of repentance: sacrifice pays a debt and that is all. The burial sites are sumptuous, the funeral furnishings are very important and the future life is considered as adjoining the life of this world. Sacrifices also serve as food for the gods, and the appetite of the divine borders on voracity if one is to judge by the masses of victuals piled up in the temples according to the priestly records. It is also necessary to feed the souls of the dead and notably to appease their thirst, otherwise they return to the earth to torment the living. In the other life the good and the bad do not seem to receive a different treatment. Warriors, however, who die honorably in battle may drink as much as they please. There is a practical morality, such as humanity unquestionably has known since its beginnings: be honest, love your parents, take care of your children, be loyal to your friends, help those who suffer, etc. . . . But this morality of the earth remains very earthly. It is dominated by a thirst for life, the sovereignly desirable good.

This is very clearly expressed in the celebrated epics of Gilgamesh and Adapa which in the ancient Orient undoubtedly played a role comparable to that of the *Illiad* and the *Odyssey* among the Greeks. The hero Gilgamesh has just lost his friend, Engidu. He feels anxiety at the idea of death, and would like to know what happens afterwards, and how to escape it if possible. He decides to go see Ut-Napishtim, the demigod who survived the deluge and whom since then the gods have kept in eternal youth in Paradise. After a thousand adventures, Gilgamesh encounters the immortal who tells him: "In the depths of the *Apsu*, there is a plant whose root is like that of the buckthorn, its thorns pierce the hand, like those of the rose, its name is "the old man becomes young." Gilgamesh plunges to the bottom of the sea and there finds the marvelous plant. But he loses it during his return journey: hence he will die, like all men. In the traditions of Eridu, one of mankind's most ancient cities, Adapa who had "broken the wings of the South Wind," was brought before the great god Anu. But deceived by Ea, he refuses the draught of life that is offered to him. Therefore he did not become immortal. This quest for immortality, this obsession to escape death, is very widespread throughout a host of myths and religions.

The pre-Islamic religions of South Arabia, so far as we can know them from inscriptions, seem terribly materialistic. Man implores the gods for a very concrete natural benefit, offers thanks for having been granted his request, and expiates faults, also very material. God is only protector, rewarder and avenger. The desert is far from being monotheist, as Renan asserted; it often seems, on the contrary, to abound in polytheism.

But the *religion of Israel* cuts violently into these Semitic religions. As a matter of fact it is permeated with Canaanite customs; for example: the Ark of the Covenant—throne of the invisible God—undoubtedly corresponds to the numerous empty thrones which archeologists have discovered in high places and where the divinity would come to seat itself. But the unique God, who revealed himself to Moses with the mysterious words, "I am is my name," is eternal, transcendent, creator, and he withdrew from men after the fall. He strikingly resembles the Great God of the origins, of whom only Israel preserved the pure image. But, and this is a very strange thing, he is worshiped and this contradicts everything we know about primitive peoples. This so-particular "ethical monotheism" prohibits sin because the omnipotent, eternal Being does not wish it (Exodus 20:5–7). As a matter of fact, there is nothing savage in the *practical* morality of the patriarchs, and that of Moses is not so very strict, but nevertheless it marks an enormous progress. Later the magnificent seeds of the Mosaic faith were to develop vigorously, instead of being smothered as in the other religions.

Greek and Roman religions, at least in their beginnings, constituted perfect examples of materialist cults. The Homeric religion was very anthropomorphic and this tendency characterized Greece: perhaps it thereby preserved itself from magic, but it barely elevated God above men. Moreover, certain philosophers, like Xenophon, protested against the likening of the divinity to men. Anonymous and blind destiny thrusts itself on humanity and on the gods. The other world is only a vague and murky abode in which semiconscious souls move about with difficulty. As the soul of Achilles says to Ulysses, after having drunk the blood of the black animals which somewhat restores his strength, "It is better to be the slave of a poor man on earth than king of dark Hades." Homer often hesitates between the conception (doubtlessly more antique) of an omnipotent Zeus and that of a god with very limited power. In any case, the souls of heroes hardly unbosom themselves to the gods; they utter only purely ritual prayers, often in an incantational form, like the supplication of Chryses to Apollo, when he traveled, after having been dismissed by Agamemnon, along "the shore of the sounding sea." It is the same in Hesiod. However, here, Dike, Justice, becomes the regulator of divine and human morality.

The Romans were on an even lower level. Their innumerable gods concerned themselves with harvests and fertility and unquestionably came straight out of the Mediterranean magma. Apart from these very indistinct deities there are some great gods among whom the most important probably is Janus, since his priest assumed the title "rex sacrorum." Jupiter appears only later. The *paterfamilias* maintains the domestic fire which burns continually and to which sacrifices are offered. They are also offered to the *Lar familiaris,* doubtlessly the guardian of the hearth, and to the Penates, deities whose role is very difficult to understand, with whom is associated Vesta, protectress of the hearth. Moreover, each member of the *gens* has his tutelary *numen* for the men, her *iuno* for the women. The cult of the dead was highly developed. They lived in peace in another world so long as they had been cremated or interred according to precise rites, and their tomb remained inviolate. It was also necessary that the father of the family continue to conduct rites in their honor on prescribed days. Moreover, they were feared: during the Lemuralia, the father of the family indulges in sinister incantations in order to expel them from his house (*Manes exite paterni*). The world beyond the grave is painted in extremely vague colors. The worship of the gods excellently expresses the Roman temperament in its juridical character: if one scrupulously fulfills the very complicated rites, without making a mistake, the divinity is obliged, as if by contract, to show itself favorable. "To each his due" would very well summarize the Roman religion. But strictly speaking, the gods (except the *Di Manes,* the divinized spirits of the dead), have no need of men.

The purely external Roman religion was not to hold out for long

when the Empire began to expand. It was too rudimentary. Not until
Plautus (in *Rudens*) was the question of evil raised in relation to
the gods. According to Ennius, if the gods do exist, they do not
concern themselves with men, otherwise the good would be rewarded
and the wicked punished. Plautus on the contrary believed that divine
justice would finally triumph and would assure the retribution of
merits. Still, these ideas must certainly have come to him as a consequence of the introduction of the Oriental cults, which had taken
place long before the time he wrote.

Cicero would seem to be a sceptic in more than one place. If he
admitted the immortality of the soul in theory, he agreed that in
practice everything ends with death. Perhaps he adhered to the
sublime ideas of the Greek philosophers, but he did not live them.
His contemporaries thought as he did, while magic and superstition
progressed (a phenomenon which always accompanies the weakening
of religion), sparing not even Sulla or Caesar. . . .

The beginnings of the *Chinese religion* have not yet been clearly
disentangled, but in it one finds a great development of the cult of
the dead with sumptuous royal tombs, human sacrifices, and divina-
tion (the Shang period, 1700–1100 B.C.). It is only under the Chou
dynasty (1100–256 B.C.) that the devotion to the Sovereign Sky
appears. But the principal features of the religion of the Shang dynasty
persist nevertheless, with agrarian rites and sexual orgies in the
springtime, when the Wei overflows and the boys and girls "go to the
orchids." A host of natural divinities are honored, without counting
the god of the door, of the hearth, of the center of the house, etc.,
dominated by the Sovereign from On High: he reigns in his palace
of the Great Bear, surrounded by the souls of the dead whose rank
seems to correspond to the one they had on earth. But it is necessary
to complicate this very simple conception, because two distinct traditions intermingle in Chinese religious thought. Thus, the souls are
two in number, the one spiritual and the other material (Tso Chuan's
Commentary on the *Ch'un Ch'iu*, 500–400 B.C.). The material soul is
the principle of the embryonic life; the spiritual soul appears only
after birth. Since the beginning of the Chou dynasty it was believed
that the latter was the only one to reach heaven after death. The
material souls would survive for a certain time near the corpse, or in

the subterranean country of the *Yellow Sources:* this doubtlessly is the reason for the funeral furnishings, but all this seems very confused in Chinese thought. Scepticism about the immortality of the soul was very general from the end of the Chou dynasty.

The rites, performed with painstaking detail and guaranteed by the virtue of the emperor, assure the proper progression of the world and the seasons. But the emperor's mandate, which has been given to him by the Sovereign Sky, can be withdrawn from him in case of bad conduct. (According to the *Shu-King*).

These conceptions were to remain those of the philosophers: Confucius makes no pronouncements on metaphysics, he is only a moralist. Even Lao-Tzu, a philosopher of entirely different scope, while preaching *Tao*, an undefinable principle of being to which one is united through ecstasy, does not believe in personal immortality. Above all (a characteristic phenomenon because it must express a fundamental feature of the Chinese soul) Taoism was to degenerate into sects whose principal concern would be to prolong life and to acquire wealth, with the aid of all kinds of sorcery and drugs (among them the famous plant of life which numerous expeditions searched for on orders of the emperor). It is true that Chinese philosophy, has also produced Mou-Tzu (470–396 B.C.) to whom we shall have to return.

Japanese Shinto has only very embryonic characteristics. In it there is a dread of defilement, physical and moral (the two are not clearly separated as among the primitives). The gods have a horror of defilement, and one must purify oneself as quickly as possible by varied rites. Theft, lying and perjury are very severely punished, but murder is viewed with greater indulgence, at least in certain cases. There is a fear of the dead who come to torment the living. Later, probably under Chinese influence, a conception of a future life slightly different from the one here below came into being along with the custom of funeral furnishings.

Belief in another life existed *among the Aztecs,* but retribution and punishment did not depend on a more or less moral conduct, but on one's destiny fixed by the gods from birth. Warriors and women who died in childbirth at first accompany the sun in its course in order to reincarnate later in the body of hummingbirds to fly from flower to flower eternally. There also exists another paradise, that of Tlaloc or Tlalocan, a wondrous garden reserved, it rather seems, for tillers of the soil. But the majority of the dead end up in the dark and gloomy Mictlan, an icy region ruled by the skeleton god Mictlan-tecutli. The dead pass through it and after all kinds of torments arrive at the new hell in order to disintegrate therein and completely cease to exist. On the whole the Aztec religion, horribly bloody and particularly chaotic, is hardly imbued with theology. Yet at Texcoco, the philosopher-king Nezahualcoyotl (1418–1472) did not seem to attribute supreme power to Ometecuhtli and Omecihuatl, the primal pair, any longer, but to a supreme god without a proper name and without images, myths and adventures, who was the creator of the universe. Are we dealing here with personal meditations of Nezahaual-coyotl or with the preservation of the Great God of the origins?

We do not know very much about the practical morality *among the Mayas,* but we can derive some information from the Lacandones, who are almost pure Mayas. Their gods are very anthropomorphic and live like men, and they are distinguished only or almost only by their immortality. Good and evil principles seem to exist.

Among the Incas, the people worshiped a host of primitive gods with a confused theogony, but above all Inca, the living god. But the religion of the aristocracy was quite different: there was an only god, Pachacamac-Uiracocha, without images to whom no offerings were made because everything belonged to him. The sovereign of the Incas multiplied the marks of his respect toward him, because he knew, like the elite, that he was in no wise a god himself, but a man like the others.

The great spiritualist religions

This distinction between spiritualist and materialist religions is neither a paradox nor an artifice designed for expository purposes. There really is a difference in the atmosphere between the two groups. But it is evident that this can be due in great part to the incomplete state of our knowledge. Moreover the materialist religions did not crystalize once and for all. They often evolved in a spiritualist direction and we must now briefly examine the principal characteristics of this evolution. *Egypt* constitutes a very special case. Alongside a swarming polytheism, it seems that Egypt also knew a *religion of wise men* which—and this is a particularly interesting phenomenon—is supposed to have been traceable back to very ancient times. It is probably the religion of the wise men that appears in the *gnomic literature or maxims* which abound in extremely lofty conceptions. For example in the *Maxims of Ani* (Eighteenth Dynasty): "Men are the image of God . . . It is not the savant alone who is his image with the mass only some sort of cattle." In the *Teaching for Merikara,* "God takes account of the one who acts for him . . . Do not kill anyone in your entourage: God who knows him has entrusted him to you." In the *Teaching of Amememope* (Twenty-second Dynasty): "Poverty from the hand of God is better than wealth in a store-room." Now, according to an interesting discussion by Drioton which there is no point in reproducing here, "God" is actually used in the singular, and it would seemingly involve a conception of a single God very common in ancient Egypt. Moreover, in certain hymns, like the one to Amon Râ for example, it is a question of "God supreme who has produced himself . . . There was no other God before him . . . One is Amon who gives way to the gods . . . It is not his image which appears in the drawings. He is too mysterious for his glory to be revealed, too great to be scrutinized, too powerful to be known." According to Drioton, one could attest to a veritable monotheist doctrine in Egypt from the time of the ancient Empire. It had been preserved by scribes and sages but curiously enough it was never able to overcome the surrounding polytheism. Belatedly, under the Ptolemies, the host of gods were considered as manifestations of "The One whose name is hidden."

Everybody knows about the developments of the cult of the dead in Egypt. Many traditions, however, are mingled with it. First the corpse, surfeited with sleep, awakens and then takes his meals in his tomb. The other world very much resembles this one. One can acquire property there and even a pension from the king who rules over the shadows. But it is necessary to avoid the *second death* which can result from the lack of funeral food or from the attacks of the monsters Gabga or Rerek . . . There are *two paradises:* that of the sun, reserved for the god-Pharaoh and his courtiers to whom he can grant the particularly coveted favor of accompanying him there, and that of Osiris for common mortals. All this merges with the prosaic idea of the food which must be brought to the dead, an idea which is not necessarily older than the paradise of Osiris, himself very ancient. Before entering the paradise of Osiris, the dead person is judged by a tribunal of "forty-two gods who rule the provinces (nomes) of Egypt"; and pronounces the celebrated "negative confession" a mixture of highly moral conceptions and magic. As Hapidjefa, prince of Assiout in the Twelfth Dynasty, writes: "I made God content because he loved me, because I remembered that I had to come to God on the day of my death." Now, this belief in judgment goes as far back at least as the Fifth Dynasty.

It is hard to explain why the magnificent *Iranian religion* did not become more widespread. The most elevated ideas are often expressed therein with the clarity of a blueprint. One must do the will of the "Wise Lord," "Ahura Mazda." Good thoughts and good actions lead to paradise, but the faithful are already rewarded on this earth. The wicked go to a hell which is not eternal. The principal weakness of the Zoroastrian religion lies in its dualism; evil stems from a bad principle "born of a bad thought of the good god" but it will be defeated at the end of the world. This explanation of the problem of evil was not to satisfy the Iranians themselves for long, because it limited the power of the Single God in a most shocking manner. This was undoubtedly understood by the Magi of Iran, since above the good god and the bad god they placed "Boundless Time," Zarvan Akarana, who very much resembles Destiny. In the face of the last judgment, Zoroastrian morality recommends all the virtues, and above all honesty, uprightness, purity. Sin, even when involuntary, must be expiated by material purifications. Too much stress perhaps is placed on rewards in the other world, forgetting, to a slight extent, disinterested love as a motive of action.

As regards *Israel*, it is known how the idea of God was purified in it, especially from the time of the great prophets and of David the Psalmist. Samuel already says: "For man seeth those things that appear, but the Lord beholdeth the heart." (1 Samuel 16:7), and Deuteronomy insists on the duty of loving God with all of one's heart and with all of one's strength. The notion of the expiatory suffering of the Just One appears in the Deutero-Isaiah. The God of the Psalms is eternal, transcendent, immovable, ubiquitous, omniscient and omnipotent. He is invisible and it is a sacrilege to ascribe a human visage to him. The Psalmist detests sin and knows that God is not content with appearances. Prayer must extend up to disinterested offering, "As the hart panteth after the fountain of water; so my soul panteth after thee, O God." (Psalm 41). But the idea of the other life remains vague and there is hardly a presentiment of it: it is here below that one must expect reward and punishment. However, in the same Psalm cited above the verse continues: "My soul has thirsted after the strong living God; when shall I come and appear before the face of God," which can perhaps be interpreted as a passionate desire to come to heavenly contemplation in the other life. Also to be recalled is the resurrection of the dead in Isaias and Ezechiel. Later, the Rabbis were to understand that the earth does not suffice for divine punishments and that it is in the world beyond that justice will be done more exactly (2 Maccabees 7:9, 14, 29, 36; 12:38, 40).

Greece, whose first thinkers, as we have seen, denounced the insufficiency of the childish divinities of Homer, was not for long to confine herself to their adoration. But wise men and philosophers are convinced intellectualists. And this is the reason why we shall not accord them the place which is usually theirs in the traditional treatises. The path which they pursued is full of nobility and grandeur. In part it established the foundations of our thought, but it does not lead us where we want to go.

It is through reasoning that Xenophon rises to the first principle, uncreated, imperishable, nonanthropomorphic. The same is true of Parmenides. Empedocles adds to similar ideas the notion of metempsychosis and the prohibition of eating meat. According to Socrates, truth, an unchanging order, and eternal types of perfection must exist somewhere, otherwise the world is absurd, life has no meaning, and morality has no foundation. He asserts the immortality of the soul, metempsychosis, reward in the future life, and Providence. For him virtue blends with knowledge. It is better to submit to injustice than to commit it and, above all, nothing is worse than to live in such a state without expiation. The only true values are the inner ones: beauty, wealth, reputation count for nothing.

In *Phaedo* Plato imagines a progressive purification of the souls in Tartarus and Phlegethon. He alludes (in the story of *Er* of Pamphylia) to a later reincarnation. In *Phaedrus* it is the progressive vision of the divinity which will decide the fate of the soul in *the future life*. Later, the incarnate soul will more or less confusedly recall it, and it will be able to ascend to Zeus himself through the disinterested contemplation of beauty. After having attacked the ridiculous fables which dishonor religion, Plato declares that God, being good, cannot be the cause of evil.

According to the Cynics, like Antisthenes, the goal of life is happiness, which is identified with virtue. Vice is identified with evil and pain. Virtue consists in the uprightness of the will and is taught only by training (an idea which goes entirely in the direction of a scientific conception). The wise man must detach himself from everything.

Aristippus and the Cyrenaics identify happiness with pleasure, the sovereign good. But it must be procured with discernment, in order to avoid future disadvantages.

For Aristotle happiness is impossible without certain minimal external conditions. Contrary to the assertions of the Cynics, the wise man cannot be happy in the bull of Phalaris or in the condition of Priam. It would also be false to identify virtue with the knowledge of good as does Socrates. It does not suffice to know it in order to practice it.

Epicurus maintains that all pain can be surmounted, even that regarded as intolerable. It is enough to recall former joys with sufficient intensity, with the help of an appropriate training. Death is not to be feared, since once the soul dissolves it can feel nothing whatsoever. Pleasure, accompanied with discernment, is the aim of life.

The *Stoic doctrines* are very much different. The wise man is conscious of the law of Zeus, and knows that happiness consists in attaching oneself to it. After the final burning, his soul will merge with that of Zeus while that of the wicked will be dispersed with no hope of return. The most important point is to maintain rectitude in one's intentions. Although the existence of evil is not denied, it must be admitted that it is undoubtedly the condition of a much greater good. It seems, as Plato said, that certain beneficent realities could not exist unless they are accompanied by painful conditions. God is propitious, benevolent, he loves men and has given them all that he could give. Virtue and happiness are nontemporal states to which duration adds nothing: An hour in the life on an honest man can equal the beatitude of Zeus. Virtue is acquired, and requires training, although Chrysippus adds that a radical evil must exist at the base of our being which education does not eliminate completely. The wise man must also extirpate all passions—even pity which is considered as one of them. He then becomes wholly perfect, indifferent to evils, omniscient, always virtuous, useful to everybody and ever joyous even in the bull of Phalaris. Death being in itself indifferent, the wise man can procure it by himself in case of necessity or even if he merely deserves it.

The mysteries

But Greek religion and morality are not limited to a few great names. For all too long now we have been entertaining an oversimple image of the Hellenic world, as guided by pure reason, and which is symbolically expressed by the impassive and radiant goddess Athena. The mysteries have been too much neglected. A whole side of the Greek soul lies at Delphi and Eleusis. But let us not lightly set the twilight, agrarian, chthonian side of the Greek spirit against its luminous, solar and rational face seen in the rise of philosophy. I have already dwelt many times on the vanity of such categories so distinctly cut off from each other. There are no such clear barriers in the domain of motivation, but the categories inextricably partake of each other. There is "reason" in Eleusis, and something other than pure reason in Plato: why for example does he attach so much importance to the Delphic oracle in the *Laws* and *Epinomis*?[4]

It is very probable that the Eleusinian mysteries started out from the very old agrarian fertility rites. Now we know that having drunk the *kukeon* the sacred objects which the mystae handled in the *kiste* (chest) and the *kalathos* (basket) were nothing else but the effigies of sexual organs. But the initiation rose to greater heights: the display of an ear of grain (perhaps the symbol of the first grain of wheat given by Demeter to Triptolemus) is not easy to interpret, but it is

---

[4]Regarded as an appendix to the *Laws* [Trans. note].

possible that we may see a symbol of resurrection there. The sublime doctrine of Eleusis, accompanied by different physical trials, produced an indelible impression on the initiated. The mysteries were always respected by the ancient Greeks, and the divulging of their secrets was punished by death. Undoubtedly it offered the soul precisely what it lacked, namely a certainty, a precise motivation which it did not find in the abstract speculation of the philosophers. The ancient Greeks had perceived, before Bergson, that the God of the philosophers has only a distant relation with the true God, known by man since the beginning and perhaps always.

Paganism at the threshold of the Christian era corresponds to the culmination of an entire series of internal stirrings which bring it very close to the Christian message. The first Christian apologists claimed that this ripening was part of the divine plan. Plutarch (*De Iside et Osiride*) alludes to ancient traditions, declaring: "The thought of the Intelligible, of the Absolute, of the Pure is like a flash of lightning . . . which allows a beautiful day to come into contact [with the Soul of the World] and to get a closer look of it. This is why Plato and Aristotle call epoptic that part of philosophy through which those who, thanks to reasoning, have gone beyond that which is opinion, mixed, diversified, and who in one leap have arrived at this first, simple, immaterial element; and in contact with the pure truth . . . they say to themselves, as one obtains the final degree in an initiation, I have Philosophy." Plutarch also alludes to Socrates' daemon who becomes almost a guardian angel in his writings. Epictetus, a very strongly religious man, at the approach of death prays to Zeus with Christian accents, "Thou re-calleth me, I take my departure, while thanking thee without reservations for having admitted me to this great spectacle of the world. I thank thee for having made me to be born. I thank thee for the other gifts. Take them back and doeth with them as thou pleaseth. They were thine, for it is from thee that I had them."

The spiritualist evolution in the other religions

The history of Roman paganism is hardly different from that of Greek paganism. But one could say that the Roman religion surrendered more quickly and more totally to scepticism and to integral materialism, without being so greatly compensated by the mysteries after the crumbling of the traditional values, like the Greeks.

It is more difficult to distinguish an evolution in the *Chinese Ocean*. But a shortsighted materialism collided not only with the currents coming from India but with Taoism. We must not forget the isolated, but so engaging, figure of Mou-Tzu who did not believe in blind fate, but posited free will, adored the omniscient and rewarding Sky, and preached universal love which must go as far as the sacrifice of one's self for one's neighbor. His following was *practically nil* and his very own pupils quickly forgot Love in order to indulge in casuistry.

In Japan the old Shinto waned very quickly (not perhaps on the political but on the religious plane) in the face of Buddhism which the Japanese mentality was to modify in a characteristic fashion. Let us pass over the sects like Tendai, Shingon and especially Zen, all of which sought illumination and deliverance through stressing either very complicated speculations, or above all, will and action. A more interesting phenomenon (for our purposes) corresponds to the development of Amitabhaism, Amitabha (Amita) is a redeeming Buddha, introduced in China in the fourth century and whose cult must have begun in the first century. Amitabha saves men who place their trust in him. He makes them attain the Pure Land (Paradise). The aim of prayer is not to petition for certain goods: it is rather an act of trust and gratitude. It is not always easy to determine the part Christian influences played in Amitabhaism.

Conclusions

I have undertaken this rapid excursion[5] through the history of religions only with the aim of *isolating,* if possible, *certain general characteristics of motivation which are expressed in religious ideas.* Man, confusedly sensing what is necessary in order for him to act

[5]The reader perhaps will be surprised to see the religion of Mohammed neglected. But in so rapid a survey of the different religions, his doctrine does not seem to be of a sufficient originality to warrant dwelling upon. It is, as everybody knows, a secondary formation. The religions of India are, on the contrary, so important that I shall examine them in a *special* chapter.

and what his actions imply, secretes a religion. *Or rather it is not he, but the species that does it.* And that is quite a different thing. But what does this mean?

1) First, *a development*, a *formalization of primitive ideas.* In the very important religions that have sufficed men for millenia, one sees only the earth. It is on this earth that benefits are obtained or where the gods fulminate their punishments. Prayers implore, and sacrifices expiate or demand their just retribution. It is the gesture correctly carried out which counts and not intention or purity of heart. Life constitutes the supreme value, and the principal role of the gods is to thrust aside death, to protect the faithful. The idea of a higher all-powerful protection, as Bergson asserts, removes all inhibitions from action. There exists another life: An absolutely universal idea in which all men have believed. But along with it go many mists and terrors. It is rarely ever conceived as happy, and the dead are often feared. In short, humanity in its youth attended to the most pressing things first: in its *thirst for action,* it acquired the motive powers for it.

2) Is that all? Quite the contrary! We have distinguished two currents among the primitives, one strictly materialist, the other which is linked to the Great God. We see this double current, perhaps, emerge again in the written religions. In the ancient Egyptian religion the only God appeared, from the first, in very pure features, while getting on well together with very different religious concepts. Moreover I believe that Schmidt was wrong in wanting to make it anterior to all the rest. It might have very well appeared *at the same time* as did all sorts of explanatory myths. But it is already very curious that it is simply there . . . The Great God is father, he is good, he makes no distinction between the poor and the rich. There is a paradise (let us recall the antiquity of the paradise of Osiris) to which no access is gained except after psychostasia, itself very ancient just as is the negative confession. The human mind must have formed spiritualist and materialist conceptions at the same time, without ever forgetting the one or the other. Israel was to make herself conspicuous by wanting to follow the only Yahweh, and yet abandoning him often for one of the many Baals . . .

3) Judging according to the present state of our knowledge it is, on the contrary, only in a very late phase that the notion of the soul panting after God like the hart after the fountain appears, and that the Great God emerges from his relative abstraction. It was also rather late that life beyond the grave—except among the Egyptians— became as important or more important than the present one. Still later, the first mystics were to discover that it is necessary to sacrifice everything on this earth, especially when He who is to come, He who will return, appears on the borders of Judea . . .

Then the human race will have ended its quest by the discovery of all that which its motivation implies. The quest and discovery will have been only in part clear and distinct, only in part rational in the traditional sense of the word reason; it will have been partially "instinctive," perhaps brought on by the mysterious thrust which moves evolution toward more psyche. Has man secreted reasons to live? Or has he discovered his essence? And are these two expressions so different from one another?

Some directions for research

It is curious to note the relative rarity of data on the theotropic function in our time, compared to the abundance of material gathered in prehistory and history. I mean that we have a great quantity of monographs dealing with the saints, and many general studies on the religious feeling. We may also cite, despite the controversies which it has aroused, Kinsey's study on the sexual behaviour of the American male. Undoubtedly the sampling is debatable and it is hardly probable that the characteristics described by Kinsey correspond in fact to the average American. They apply rather to a certain class of newly-arrived and fairly demoralized immigrants. But this study remains a model of *descriptive morality,* very close to our subject. It is completely irrational, I repeat, to discuss human motivation *ad infinitum,* if we do not know what it is *in fact,* what the acts considered licit or illicit are *in reality: In reality* means the acts really committed or avoided with a *measurable* frequency. Let us also cite Le Bras' so interesting school of religious sociology which heads exactly in the direction that interests us here.

For if it is of greater importance, as I will point out later on, to study the theotropic function at its maximum intensity with heroes and saints, one cannot neglect its origin, nor even its degenerations:

for everything can enlighten us on what it really is. It seems to constitute an integral part of man, who can only make believe dispensing with it. This ends up in solidly rooting theology in ethnography and psychology. The study of the development of the idea of God and of the moral law, which can be separated only in theory, must be conducted according to the same rules as the study of the evolution of the nervous system. This is not to degrade a science whose devotees would prefer to keep in the empyrean, but it does provide that science with an objective basis which it has lacked a bit too long.

Let us not confuse it, however, with the two sciences we have just mentioned, for its object is quite different: it studies, or should study, the relations between moral and religious theories and the acts of the *moral world* in current life. And it strives to evaluate the degree of success of its theories. Obviously I mean success in an objective sense by taking happiness, stability, in a word the efficacy which man has always sought—as criteria. How do men react to evil, to suffering, to death? How is this type of reaction linked to their theopathic armature? We hardly know, and it would be so important to learn! Here the axis of interest shifts from that of the ethnologist. Primitive societies, properly so called, are less interesting to us because they are little intellectualized, and because their motivations are often too rudimentary. They can content themselves with moral forms which correspond to a former and surpassed stage of humanity, the stage when men posed no, or few, problems to themselves. This is to say that the degenerate forms of contemporary religious societies, or their offshoots, their deviations etc. seem more important to us than primitive societies. What is the lack, felt in the motivation, which produces separation from one faith and adherence to another? The sprouting of new sects, so frequent in America, the attempts to introduce strange religions in the white man's society, would be the preferred object of study for the new theology.

In a word, ethnology and the history of religions are descriptive sciences. Theology, as one might conceive it—in addition to its perennial tasks—would undertake a more dynamic aim, closer to experimental sociology: To understand the operation (rather than the geography) of those religious organs which humanity gives itself, and the study of the products of their metabolism.

Part II

Up to now I have attempted to gather some materials of a scientific order on religion, morality, and motivation. I have done as best I know how, as best could be done by a biologist whose competence is not universal, but who feels the urgency of these questions and the personal and ineluctable necessity of studying them. Let us now try to go further, to arrive at the paths which will lead to a decision: A decision on the motivational plane, which is that of action, rather than on the *purely* discursive plane. Then the *decision leads to an experiment,* which it is important to carry out under ideal conditions. And according to whether it succeeds or not, the laboratory worker will adhere or not to a specific religious (motivational) system.

In my opinion, the conditions of the experiment are simplified because there now exist only two great modern religions worthy of interest: The Christian religion and the religious complexes of India. Let us examine them as best as we can in order to decide whether the experiment has more chances of success in one or the other case. I shall be very brief in regard to the Christian religion, because I shall return to it later, and notably in connection with Brahma and Buddha.

4

The Christian Religion

I believe that the expositions of the religion of Christ, such as are made by its priests, are sometimes so confused that one understands nothing of them. Not because they are lacking in sublime ideas, but because they are expressed in a language unadapted to our epoch. So much so that many good people, devoured by metaphysical anxiety, and who could find peace in Christianity, turn away from it because they have taken the accessory for the essential.

Let us therefore try to follow the Christian religion back to some simple idea-forces, such as they are *lived* each day by the Christian worthy of this name.

The method

It may appear fastidious to insist each time on method. However, I believe that it must be done. The fact is that from the start we encounter a reef that is all the more dangerous because it is inconspicuous. In the examination of a religion, traditional reason would insist upon a return to historical sources which would be submitted to a searching critique. One would then pass on to an examination of the development of the doctrine, verifying at each time whether it corresponds properly to the basic postulates. Finally it would be necessary to determine whether its claims to truth have some chance of being established from a philosophical point of view.

Now, in my opinion, to proceed in this way is an *appalling error*. It is to withdraw oneself from all chances of ever succeeding. The reader will understand this in accordance with what I have just said in the preceding pages: Religion is lived rather than demonstrated.

Without a previous experience the most beautiful demonstrations in the world do not touch the total man. Through it these demonstrations acquire all their force of attraction: "No man can come to me, except the Father, who has sent me, draw him" (John 6:44).

Consequently, I shall give all eventual adversaries a chance. I concede all the stupidities, all the crimes of which the men of the Church have been guilty since the beginning. I grant all the obscurities of the Scriptures and the subtle discussions of the exegetes. All this, provided that you acknowledge the existence of saints and martyrs of sterling quality, and acknowledge that the Scriptures *also* contain passages of a beauty so sublime that they constitute the patrimony of all humanity. Hence to all the contra arguments, one can oppose a pro argument. Once more we encounter the undecidable. Let us recall then the first pages of this book: The undecidable is the evident sign that a question must be approached by another method, and that the one which has been followed simply does not work. How can we go forward then? By studying the nature of the message, the kind of experiment which it permits us to set up, the success or failure of this experiment: That is to say its degree of conformity with reality. Now, has a message been transmitted which allows us to begin this experiment? Incontestably yes, and everybody admits it, although it has often been distorted in a hundred ways.

The Christian message

The existence of a personal God, distinct from the world, of an infinite power, for whom the entire universe with its dimensions that confound the imagination is naught but a grain of dust.

This God interests himself prodigiously in man, in each man in particular. He came formerly among us, in order to teach us to follow his way, but without violating our freedom, hence without making use of his power: Infinite in his love, as he is in all, he wished to suffer and die for us. The true reason thereof is inaccessible to man (the mystery of the Incarnation and of the Resurrection), for it touches upon the unfathomable divine nature and on the inscrutable relations between God and man. One can, however, form for himself a *rudimentary* idea of the motives of the Sacrifice: It seems that Christ wished to introduce us directly into the mysterious universe of the reversibility of merits (see below) and therefore teach us to suffer for others with a perfect generosity, as he did. And on the other hand to compensate, on the mysterious plane of expiation and justice, for the past and the future crimes of humanity. Perhaps God also wishes, when he let himself be humiliated on the cross and when he unites with man in the humble form of bread and wine, perhaps he wishes us to understand that anything excellent that we may ever do, that anything we may ever suffer, no matter how terrible, is nothing in relation to the Infinite Sacrifice.

Evil exists on earth, but it constitutes the reverse side of human freedom. It was man and not God who introduced it. God therefore permitted it, without having wished it, undoubtedly because a wicked man, as long as he is free, is infinitely superior to a saint who is not free. But God detests evil; we must fight against it with all our might, especially in its roots, which are the vices and flaws of human nature.

But evil entails sacrifice and suffering: It is here that one of the most mysterious teachings of Christianity intervenes. The consequences of all the evil and of all the good, of all the crimes and all the virtues come together as if in a great reservoir: We are happy and we suffer *all together,* for we are all jointly responsible. But God infinitely multiplies the consequences of just action which, when poured into the common reservoir, entail infinite effects. Hence each one can do everything for the others, and should do everything for them.

This must be understood *on the moral plane,* for the kingdom of God is not of this world. And the present life is but a sojourn, the reverse of a place which is elsewhere. We do not understand everything in it and will not be able to understand everything in it. But we must place our trust in God: His coming on earth is the pledge of his love for us. Human life is but a brief preparation for a higher mode of existence, for while man has had a beginning he shall have no end.

Christian faith therefore leads to an *enthusiastic adhesion to the divine order of the world,* which cannot but be the best possible one, provided man applies himself to remove, with God's help, all evil from it. Let us just for an instant measure what would be the potential dynamism of a Christian completely convinced that God interests himself in all his actions and, if they are truly good, that God confers an infinite reward on them, for him and for others.

The rewarding and avenging God

Unquestionably one of the most poorly understood aspects of the Christian doctrine is that of the rewarding of acts. What merit does the believer have since he hopes for the perfect reward of paradise? It is here that recourse must be made to the theory of religious stages according to which experience includes a series of degrees of development, from the crudest to the loftiest. To man still slumbering in a semianimal motivation, the incitements to a loftier action are known but insufficiently: In the beginning only the fear of hell and the desire for paradise provide efficient stimuli. But the invitation to go further and higher remains ever present. At the other end of the scale we find the motivation of the saints in which only the contemplation of the goodness of God and of what he has done for man determines acts: Here one tends toward the sovereign Good as the result of the attraction peculiar to it, independently of all thought of reward. Certain saints, like Teresa, go so far as to write that they would continue to love God, even in hell.

Many scientists would have it that a truly pure faith would activate men only for motives of a higher order. We think that it would not work in a great number of cases and, therefore, is not true according to our criteria. Let us add that the child learns the mechanics of the truly good action, as early as his catechism. In fact let us take a look at the French catechism:

"240. *When is your contrition perfect?* I have perfect contrition when I am sorry for my sins because sin offends God, who is infinitely good, and because it caused the death of our Lord.

"241. *When do you have imperfect contrition?* I have imperfect contrition when I am sorry for my sins because I am ashamed of having committed them or because *of fear of hell.* [My italics.]

"242. *What does perfect contrition do?* Perfect contrition forgives our sins, even before absolution, provided that we have the desire to go make a good confession.

"243. *What does imperfect contrition do?* Imperfect contrition does not forgive our sins, but it disposes us to receive the forgiveness of the sacrament of penace.

"244. *Make an act of contrition.* Oh my God I am very sorry for having offended Thee, because Thou art infinitely good and sin displeases Thee."

One will note the complete absence of any allusion to reward and punishment in the act of contrition. Now the children recite this text every day for years. Nevertheless *these same children* know of the existence of reward and punishment.

The place of man in nature

Many will be amazed by the almost exorbitant place which Christian theory accords to man in nature. Do we not find therein an anthropomorphism without a rational base? I believe rather that we are again dealing with an *undecidable:* Here the pros and contras could both be equally sustained with the help of semirational and semi-emotional arguments. On the one hand one can picture man as swallowed up in an ocean of galaxies, a fragment of an animal evolution which did not know him for millenia, and which will undoubtedly forget him again in a short time. And there are no indications that God, if he exists, concerns himself with man. But it is just as logical to claim that something new appeared with man, mind and consciousness at its highest level. And perhaps, in a certain way, the mind is equal to the ensemble of the cosmos, since it manages to conceive it. Finally, if evolution really tends toward more nervous system, that is to say towards more mind, it is probably correct to attribute a wholly particular place to man.

But none of these arguments, for or against, is fully decisive. What is it that will allow us to reach a decision if it is not, once again, the measure of the moral efficacy of one theory in relation to the other, that is to say the measure of its truth? You maintain that man is a speck of dust lost in the galaxy and without any importance whatsoever? Try then to think this seriously, to practice "ekagrata" like the Mindus, the concentration on this sole point in such a way as that it imbues all your acts which at each step deny such a conception? What will happen then? It is easy to foresee: Death or madness, or in any case a boundless despair. So much so that you cannot seriously admit the first theory and continue to live.

Still one might object that the measure of efficacy comes into play here only in relation to man, and that one cannot extend the conclusions of moral experience to the cosmos. One cannot extend anything to the cosmos, one can conclude nothing therefrom. One can decide only at our level and pick the theories that are in accord with our nature, that is to say with the shaft of time, with evolution, with something immensely greater than ourselves. This is the only truth accessible to us. Moreover, it is physically impossible for us to hold certain theories.

But once again, the place accorded the individual seems very great, if one can rigorously concede a certain importance to humanity. It is not possible to discuss this except in the vaster perspectives of the necessities of motivation and efficacy, again and always. In our civilization, at any rate, the idea of the importance of the individual so permeates our mores that it is almost impossible to submit it to question again. But we shall return to this subject a little later on.

God and morality

One will notice in this book a perpetual—and deliberate—confusion between the idea of God and moral laws. Cannot a morality without God exist? Undoubtedly it can, and the Chinese seem to have approached it. Some certainly tried to set up the reflections of certain Greek philosophers as a morality. But on the practical plane, moralities without God are, if they exist at all, an ethnographic rarity. Man does not separate the two in his acts. Hence it seems contrary to all psychology to divide in the experiment what has always seemed united. Moreover, the attempts of atheist philosophers have not gotten anywhere up to now. Or else they then introduce into their theories a host of "Christian ideas become mad" which they cannot even recognize, so imbued are they by them. Thus the Marxists sacrifice themselves, with an admirable abnegation, in the hope of reaching or letting others reach heaven (the classless society). It is a veritable *eschatology*, the coming of which for them is neither more or less evident than that of Christ at the end of time. In fact humanity may never get to such a point, or even may transform itself in thousands of years, through a series of sociological setbacks, in a way that no one can actually foresee or conceive. Finally, one can set up a host of hypotheses, and the classless society is only one of them, highly desirable but very uncertain. The same goes for the infallibility of the Party which preserves the precious "deposit of faith" intact, as well as determines the manner of making use of it. Nothing of all this is justifiable from a scientific point of view. It is a religion which is tenable only because of its Christian impregnation, so deep that its followers no longer distinguish it. They do not see to what extent their reactions are imbued with it. The Marxist theories of Action are not valid on the plane of reason. And we have better ones on the plane of religion.

The martyrs

All religions like the Marxist have had their martyrs, superb specimens of humanity in general, before whom we must reverently bow our heads. For this reason, like Pascal, is it necessary to believe *all* the tales whose witnesses let their throats be cut? Probably not. When a theory is sufficiently developed and sufficiently *disinterested*, it produces martyrs almost automatically. *This is only a test of quality.* But the degree of success, the degree of the profound adequation of a theory to motivation is a statistical datum which includes the percentage of success and the duration. From the fact that the Cathari died courageously in the flames, it does not follow that their heresy could have filled the motivational lacunae of humanity for as long, and as completely, and for so many people, as has Christianity. In a word, *it is necessary but not sufficient* for a religious or moral doctrine to produce martyrs.

Miracles

I would like to follow the same mode of reasoning in regard to miracles. These extraordinary facts, naïvely admired by the simple people, are very much disdained by scientists. They must be considered under a more subtle light. For a Catholic the fact that Christ believed it good to perform miracles will help him to admit that they must be good for something. For the unprejudiced scientist who approaches religious questions, it will seem probable that the intrusion of the Divine, of the supreme Force, can be accompanied by some unexpected phenomena on the physical plane. Hence, like the martyrs, miracles by themselves do not constitute proof of a doctrine, but only the sign that unusual concentrations of a force poorly known have manifested themselves. It remains to study them in order to discern their origin. But it would be serious lack, I believe, for a great religion to have no miracles at all.

The attitude that a scientist should observe in the presence of such facts is more properly characterized through an analysis of a recent book by J. Lhermitte on the miracle. The author is a highly esteemed neurologist and a sincere Christian. He is also—perhaps without being aware of it—a scientist full of inferiority complexes vis-à-vis science. He forgets that the God of the Christians has nothing to fear from the science which he has created along with everything else. I shall dwell on Lhermitte's book at some length because I am convinced that the scientist must in no way renounce his mentality when he is dealing with religious facts. Now, Lhermitte certainly shares the same conviction. However, as will be seen, our conclusions on the miracle are *diametrically opposed*.

My opposition is based on a different conception of science and on a different attitude in the presence of the extraordinary fact. I would like science to maintain its open-mindedness, and to become aware of its extreme youth and rid itself of the tendency to doubt an inexplicable fact *only* because it does not see how it can be integrated into one of the systems provisionally in favor.

a) It is difficult to verify a fact when it is accidental and yet it is necessary to recognize the right of extraordinary facts to exist.

One can find examples of Lhermitte's panic in the presence of an extraordinary fact, or one presumed to be so, on every page of his book.

Page 101: *The case of Mme. Bire,* affected with bilateral blindness, resulting from meningeal phenomena. Loss of sight, abolition of pupillary reflex to light, atrophy of the two pupils. Observation Dr. Lainez: "Right eye: white is pearly, pupil almost imperceptible. Left eye: white is nacreous, pupil very diminished, but nearly double that of the right eye. Despite this they hardly have a third of their normal diameter. An absolutely incurable illness." Following a visit to Lourdes, a sudden cure after receiving communion. Observation by Dr. Rubbrecht one month later: "I found no trace of the atrophy of the optic nerve described by Dr. Lainez. The pupil in both eyes has a beautiful dewy color, the pupils have their normal diameter. The pupil reacts properly to light and to accommodation: everything is normal."

Lhermitte's criticism: It was not the same ophthalmologist who examined her before and afterward. This is serious enough to regard the cure as conditional (line 8, page 102: "if such a cure has been affected.")

Page 106. *The case of Pierre de Rudder.* Open fracture of the leg overrun through years by suppuration with elimination of bony sequestra. Sudden cure following prayers to Our Lady of Lourdes.

Lhermitte's criticism: Poorly made observation on the state of the bones after the cure, with contradictions suggesting that one of the practitioners might have been mistaken about the leg involved. The contradictions in the observations are real. However that may be, I would like to see Lhermitte answer one single question instead of losing himself in osteological quibbling: Did de Rudder walk before the miracle? And did he walk afterwards? In my opinion, and perhaps also in poor de Rudder's, this is the only important point.

Page 151: *M. D. operated on by Dr. Picot.* After laparotomy, cancer of the gall bladder, considerable adhesion to the wall and to the transverse colon. Enormous sub-pancreatic ganglionic invasion with carcinosis.

The surgeon did not operate and closed the abdomen again. Further aggravation of the condition of the patient. One day he asked his wife to apply a relic of St. Thérèse to his body. Immediate improvement; resumption of feeding on the very next day; rapid recovery. Later gastrohepatic symptoms similar to the first necessitated more surgery, also made by Dr. Picot, who discovered a voluminous gall stone which he removed. But the peritoneum was without defect, smooth and regular; pancreas completely normal. Completely cured, the patient has been getting along perfectly since his operation.

M. Lhermitte's criticism: Dr. Picot (a friend of Lhermitte and who reported all these facts to him) did not make a biopsy for fear of a hemorrhage. Hence, perhaps it was not a cancer: M. Lhermitte holds that a biopsy is necessary even when cancer stares you in the face. Since I am a good fellow, I shall even suggest an explanation that he has forgotten. It happens that some cancers are considerably improved after a simple laparotomy, without any other intervention. There are well-described cases in the literature and which are otherwise totally unexplained. But here the troubles yielded not to a laparotomy, but only after the application of the relics of St. Thérèse, and immediately.

Page 146: *The celebrated case of Marie Ferrand, observed by Carrel.* In the train en route to Lourdes, Carrel observed Marie Ferrand, affected with tubercular peritonitis. He made a detailed observation of her abdomen, informed himself about her tubercular history, and tried to sustain her somehow with the help of caffeine and mitigate her suffering with some morphine. She arrived in agony at the grotto. Carrel saw her stomach lose its swelling before his eyes and thought he was going mad. The miracled woman immediately began to take food. A thorough examination was made on the following morning by two other doctors. All signs of the peritonitis had disappeared, the patient wanted to get up from bed.

M. Lhermitte's criticism: He feels "almost" obliged to conclude that Marie Ferrand really did suffer from tubercular peritonitis. But just the same Carrel could have been mistaken (yes, but at that very moment?) and then one doesn't know what became of Marie Ferrand afterward. Did her recovery continue? (if by chance there had been a relapse, would the fact observed by Carrel thus become undoubtedly entirely natural?)

In these several examples one will see precisely where Lhermitte's error lies. When an extraordinary and inexplicable fact is attested to by witnesses worthy of credence, one must accord its credence. Unless, like our author, one makes a particularly clumsy use of historical criticism, and demands from history an *absolute certainty* which not even the natural sciences can provide, with the exception of mathematics. On the other hand when there is only a slight chance of error in the diagnosis, the alleged fact becomes strongly *probable*, and not *improbable*.

Now, Lhermitte's constant procedure consists in insisting that a fact is doubtful when it does not exhibit the characteristics of absolute certainty. One would like to know whether he often meets in his own medical practice the certainty of which he is so enamored. This procedure is so generally employed in his book that it would give rise to doubts about the author's good faith if everyone were not so aware of his moral rectitude. The distinguished professor simply poses pseudoproblems and reasons the wrong way.

In an extremely strict sense, if a *single* extraordinary *fact* was produced at Lourdes or elsewhere, and if, as happens always with an unexpected fact, the controls were not as rigorously applied as they should have been, one would be able to understand the suspension of judgment about the reality of the fact. But what is one to do if a whole series of such facts is produced?

b) It is false that God is frightened by X-rays or any kind of human controls.

At least different methods of improving the controls could be organized at Lourdes. It is not impossible to foresee a procedure organized whereby each patient, before going to the pool, will be subjected to a very detailed examination with the aid of the most modern techniques. This, at least, is what any man of good sense would propose in order to calm Lhermitte's last scruples.

Now here our author adopts a position that I cannot understand: he does not insist on verifications that are too precise because then there would be no more miracles (pp. 131–132). Well, now! the reader will exclaim, here is a declared confession, an absolute refusal to believe in miracles? I don't think so, or at least this allergy to miracles exists only in Lhermitte's subconscious. But "to act too scientifically would be to make oneself judge of God" (p. 132) and so, Lhermitte calls Richelieu to the rescue by citing one of the possessed nuns of Loudun whose allegations the latter refused to have verified. Then follow a certain number of pages in which Lhermitte has not at all succeeded in convincing me that God is afraid of our miserable human controls. If such were the case Christ would have never counseled the healed lepers to go show themselves to the priests. At the third or fourth reading, it seemed to me, however, that I could discern a feeble light: If the author wishes to say that science, despite all its techniques, in the presence of an extraordinary fact will never be able to assert that it involves a miracle signed by God, I am in full agreement with him. Science can only declare: Here is a fact that it is impossible to explain in the state of our knowledge, but it has really been produced and it is impossible to doubt it. But is this really the author's thought?

c) Our Lord has put himself in a very bad position by not letting his miracles be witnessed by a delegation of the Academy of Medicine.

Despite his exaggerated scepticism, Lhermitte, who is a very sincere Christian, declares that he accords full credence to the miracles of the Gospel, because he says (p. 57) "one of the essential characteristics which sets the marvelous and the prodigious apart from the authentic miracle is that the latter conceals a lesson in itself and possesses a moral value." Evidently, if God permits a miracle it must be because it serves some purpose. For example, the extraordinary healing of Marie Ferrand was perhaps not devoid of moral significance, since from then on Carrel began to revise his metaphysical positions. And one cannot very well see why miracles, useful in evangelical times, should lose all their moral efficacy and all their power to induce conversion in our time, when a hundred examples prove the contrary.

But I am above all amazed that Lhermitte does not sense how incompatible it is to demand verifications, so elaborate that they become absurd, for a miracle in our day, and to blindly accept the miracles of the Gospel (or the stigmata of St. Francis, p. 136). Every unbeliever will feel the howling contradiction such a position implies. Lhermitte consents to forgive Christ, because he is God, the indecency involved in not subjecting himself to the laws of nature. But since there now exists a functioning Academy of Medicine, God should understand of himself, unless he wants to behave like a dangerous revolutionary, that he must not sadden this venerable institution with the help of tricks of a dubious taste.

Is it not more reasonable to admit that God, in all his power, performed miracles before, performs them now and will perform them later, whenever his wisdom esteems them useful? And from the moment they are verified by witnesses worthy of faith who have used sufficient precautions, the scientist must admit that an extraordinary fact has occurred—and the believer should perhaps bend his knee before the miracle.

d) Lhermitte has formed an idea of science that is too proud and too absolute.

More than one scientist—Lhermitte included—seems to retain a conception of determinism that is a little too absolute. "The deniers [of miracles] . . . declare they cannot conceive of the possibility of an interference in the ineluctable sequence of causalities . . . and they maintain a very strong position" (p. 164). "If on the contrary one admits that the principle of determinism is only relative and leaves room for manifestations whose link with their antecedents is not exactly grasped—then a breach is opened in the doctrine of determinism and one no longer has the power to stem the rising tide of arbitrary manifestations" (p. 158).

In the face of the serious confusion manifest in these two sentences, it is necessary to return for a moment to the concept of the law of nature and determinism on which science is actually based. First of all we must not have too juridical a conception of these laws: *there are no laws,* but only findings of a statistical order. In that which we have been able to observe up to now, phenomena occur in such a way that an equation can summarize a phenomenon in the abbreviated language of mathematics (but not *codify* it). Determinism expresses the belief that everything has a cause and that behind phenomena there are no malicious demons capable of perverting them in an unforeseeable way. This conception cannot embarrass or distress any believer, provided that the scientists concede that things occur in this way *only in the greatest majority of cases.* If, by chance, one time out of a million water did not freeze at 32°F, nothing would be changed in current physics. A new phenomenon would be noted and it would be necessary to sift out the cause (which would be practically impossible if the occurrence is too rare). If one does not succeed in doing this, the physicists will not die of despair over it. In the case of special phenomena of the miraculous type, the believer need not abjure his determinist convictions, but only admit that the laws of nature have been suspended or thwarted by an external cause (the will of God). If God worked miracles every five minutes, all science would be in fact impossible. But at the rate God maintains, science and religion can painlessly coexist.

Moreover Lhermitte completely admits such a position (p. 165). After which he adds (p. 165), God knows why, that a miracle is an event whose thread the scientist "cannot disentangle in principle . . . For if the biologist succeeded in ferreting out its genesis," he could undoubtedly some day reproduce the phenomenon and it would no longer be a miracle. As far as I am concerned if some scientist succeeds in knowing to the minutest detail what happened in Pierre de Rudder's leg, he would see only that at a certain moment the kinesis of the reactions and even their type took another course. And why, in fact, would he not succeed in reproducing the phenomenon, aided by all the means of future science? And yet there was still a miracle that did occur at Lourdes on a certain day, in which God achieved in an instant what man would later copy more or less laboriously. Let us not confuse the extraordinary with the impossible, nor with the absurd.

By the intervention of God a *material* process is modified. What's so amazing about the scientist one day discovering the point of insertion of divine action on matter? Must God act in a manner incomprehensible to man for there to be a miracle?

e) An attitude like Lhermitte's is prejudicial to science. Nothing could more effectively hamper progress than a timorous trust in the principles of the sciences, a jealous insistence upon closing one's eyes before what seems to contradict these principles. Our laws are provisional; one single thing is certain: our grandchildren will laugh at them. Nothing is more noxious than to want to lead the unknown precipitately to the known, by explaining the obscure by means of the obscure: For example, "faith healing" about which we know practically nothing, or group suggestion, about which our ignorance is almost complete, cannot be invoked lightly in order to render a miraculous fact more plausible. At the end of his book, Lhermitte cites with praise the works of Brosse and Laubry on the yogis of India who are capable of commanding their musculatory and their nervous systems in a way that a Westerner finds incredible. Brosse, however, has at his disposal irrefutable records showing that the alleged prodigies have taken place. What would she have discovered if she had shown the same scepticism that Lhermitte affects a little further on in connection with the phenomena of levitation? I believe, moreover, that the study of miracles would sometimes be able to put us in the presence of traces of divine action, and would unquestionably often supply us with other eminently interesting facts (of Brosse and Laubry type). Is it known, for example, that the Hindus believe that a god can die, that is to say become inefficacious when the fervor of the faithful has for a long time not recharged him with energy (prana) which he redistributes afterwards? I don't know whether or not prana exists, but I sometimes ask myself whether certain healings attributed to relics cannot be interpreted in this fashion. Such a study remains to be done (see Thurston especially).

The absolute impartiality of the scientist consists in being neither for nor against, in renouncing without regret the synthesis of which one was so proud the day before, in order to enter a period of uncertainty, from which one will emerge only by accepting another equally provisional synthesis. Here is a very arduous task, but that which falls on the shoulders of us scientists . . . And which will perhaps allow us to recognize him or his traces as did Elias, in another time, on Mount Carmel.

5

Brahma and Buddha:
The Systems of Oriental
Thought

We have already agreed on the particular importance of the religions of India. For my part I have always thought that there were only two systems worthy of study in the world: Christianity and the religions of India. Without wishing to ignore the importance and originality of diverse parallel theories (like Zen and Tao), let us agree that they belong to the same type as Hinduism. They are steeped in the same atmosphere. Unquestionably we shall not commit too grave an error by attaching ourselves only to the thought of India here, since the other religions of the Far East differ from it only in their nuances.

Truth to tell, the analysis from the outset presents two very arduous difficulties: In order to discuss a religious system with justice, it is necessary to have lived it, as we have seen and will see again. I have never followed Brahma or Buddha. Hence I can speak only roughly of the effects of their faith on the chemistry of the act. And this for the same reasons that a nonphysicist will deal with physics only from the outside. However, a very great effort of popularization has already been carried out for many long years by more or less scientific orientalists. Who would deny our present familiarity with India which differs enormously from the practical ignorance of the last century? Now a large public is interested in yoga, karma, and in a hundred words, sonorous and rich in vowels, which it employs at random. But, it is especially annoying to hear people express amazement before a foreign wisdom because it is presented to them by curious, ardent-eyed personages in yellow robes, while they are curiously unconcerned to deepen the old religion of the West, or even to practice the rudiments thereof. Hence a restatement of these oriental religious systems —fully acknowledging as we do its approximate character—will certainly not be useless.

But then a second and more serious difficulty arises: The doctrines of India are like the sea itself. Everything perhaps would be found at the bottom of this metaphysical abyss. The strangest theories,[1] as well as the most wise principles (to which a Christian could adhere) have not lacked sectarian followers. So much so that scarcely can one affirm that a characteristic is peculiar to the Hindu mentality, though an opposite assertion may be made with equal authority. It seems, however, that a guiding thread can tie everything together. Very soon after the Vedic period, and ever since the first Upanishads, the concept of the wheel of life became explicit. It involves the soul in innumerable transmigrations, until it has exhausted the poison of its previous acts. For the rest, this life is but an illusion, the important thing is to get out of it definitively and to merge with the universal Self, or rather to realize that one is and always has been naught else than *One* with it. Different techniques for achieving deliverance, different conceptions of the value of acts, of asceticism and of sacrifices were elaborated around these fundamental ideas. But, as someone has profoundly observed, these differences have no more importance than those of the religious orders within Christianity. This is why they lasted so easily, since after all they were at bottom in agreement with each other. Hence if one does not go into detail, it must be possible to isolate the few idea-forces which will suffice for our purpose.

Let us therefore briefly summarize the principal features of the Hindu view of the world.

The creation of the world

The Hindu concept of cause is not at all the same as with us; at least it does not have the same genesis. In the West, one might grant that it derives from the sensation of muscular effort: I push an object and I feel myself to be the cause of its fall. In India, as in Babylon, it is

---

[1] Even atheism and disrespect for the Holy Writings: One Hindu school taught that the Vedas were but "the drivel of a drunk."

rather the idea of generation, of descent in the sense of procreation which constitutes the framework. It seems that at this level we already find an opposition of temperaments, which we shall later have to stress many times.

Hence, at the beginning is found the cause of causes, the neuter Brahma, about which one can say nothing because it is beyond all expression and inconceivable for a man of the usual type. Let us here incidentally recall a phrase of St. Thomas: "If somebody says that God is, in the sense in which man is, then it is better to say that God is not." The Hindus do not believe in a creation *ex nihilo*. "How would being be born of nothing?" asks the Chandogya Upanishad. For that matter Christians do not believe in this either. But Brahma— or God—at the beginning is not nothingness. Certain Christian theologians tend to replace creation by relation: matter, in its existence and its mode of being depends on God, and not conversely.

The universe therefore is born of a thought of Brahma. But how can the Many be born of the One? But isn't this sudden change an attack on the majesty of the Single? Denis de Rougemont has very clearly seen that this difficulty, so often envisaged by the Greeks, had been a very passionate preoccupation of the Hindus. Is it necessary then to sacrifice the One—and consider its existence as an idle question—or must the Many be sacrificed? Indian philosophy adopted the latter decision. The Many cannot exist, it can only *seem to be;* it is maya, illusion. As Krishnachandra Bhattacharya says, "the world is an absolute appearance, at once real and unreal; real as Brahma, as cause which continues in its effect, and unreal in that it is different from it." On the other hand, however, human misery forces us to take leave from maya and, says Ramakrishna (1834-86), "it is only thanks to maya that the conquest of Supreme Wisdom and of the Ultimate Beatitude has been possible to us. . . . Without maya, how would we have been able to know Brahma?" So much so that the Hindu systems all tend to monism. Herbert has rightly pointed this out. But one can easily conceive nonduality (advaita) or at least "realize" it practically.

Here is an important point on which I feel myself entirely in agreement with the Hindus. This whole book proves it. Merely to conceive a philosophy, they say, is nothing. In some way or another it must be possible to experience it, to live it. If Western philosophy

is in a state of distinct decline and bogged down in verbalism, is it
not because it has abandoned our only mistress, experience?

Still, it is the difficulty of realizing unity that makes many Hindus
dualists in practice.

Brahma-Atman

This eternal, immovable, and impassible Brahma is but one with
atman, the individual soul. We do not only participate in the divine
nature, as Christians say, we are this very nature itself; there is but
one aim in life, to succeed in recognizing it, in realizing it. In fact,
our feelings and our mind, the fruits of maya, step in between and
hide from us the true atman. There is something beyond the mind,
which is Mind. There exists a dormant faculty which permits man
to escape time, matter, suffering, and which he must awaken. No
sacrifice, no austerity would be too hard in order to arrive at this
goal. When one has rightly understood this, one has touched the very
depths of the Hindu soul.

From this point of view, Buddha introduces differences of technique
rather than a fundamental revolution in the doctrine. Under the fig
tree of knowledge he discovers that neither privations nor asceticism
lead to deliverance if, in the heart of the adept, there still subsists the
desire to live, the father of sorrow and illusion. This is what the
blessed one declared in the course of his celebrated sermon to the
Djatilas, who celebrated the Agnihotra sacrifice by immersing themselves completely nude in the icy river. And the Djatila, Ourouvela
Kassapa, admitted this without too much difficulty, perhaps because
he pursued the same aims as the Buddha, so that it was not worth
the trouble to quarrel too passionately over differences in itineraries.

This obsession with life that must be dried up characterizes Hindu
religion. It involves several consequences. First of all, the absence
of any fear of death: Birth and death constitute phenomena as frequent as sleeping and waking, and about which there is no reason
to be troubled. *It is life* that constitutes a troublesome trial and of
which it is proper to quit oneself as quickly as possible.

Let us pause here for a moment. I believe this point is fundamental.
Nothing is more different to the Western soul: Let us recall the fierce

love of life in Sumer, Babylonia, Israel, and among the Greeks. It is true that in the Gospel, the kingdom of God is not of this world. But this world is nevertheless the excellent work of the Only God, in which man alone—and not creation by its very nature—introduced evil. As it issued forth from divine hands, the world was worthy of love and an object of delight. The stories of the earthly paradise and the very term eternal *life* are entirely characteristic. And, did I not fear the anathema of fiery Indianizers like Jean Herbert, I would put forward the notion that Vedas are not so impregnated with a despairing concept of the world. I am thinking of certain canticles which overflow with a cosmic joy, and in particular of the magnificent hymn to the earth of the Atharvaveda (XII, II):

"To the Earth belong the four horizons, nourishment and labors are born of her. All that breathes and vibrates she bears in many ways. May the earth grant us oxen and abundance!

"Bearer of all things, receptacle of the good, dwelling, breast of gold, it is she which halts that which walks and she who sustains the universal fire. India is her bull. May the earth wish to establish us in riches!

"Universal generatrix, mother of plants, immovable and vast earth which keeps the law. Pacific, hospitable: may we walk along her for ever!

"Immense shelter, you are the immense, immense is thy trembling, thy tumult, immense India who guards thee without fail. Let us shine, o earth, like under the reflection of gold!"

Evidently, the Upanishads were to bend religion toward more arid views. And I do not ignore the fact that the Hindus, thanks to frantic efforts at interpretation, were to claim that all these things were but one and the same doctrine. But if the effort of the sages has succeeded in deriving some admirable speculations from the hymns which were sung by some robust Aryan priest, it is because one can derive anything from a text, by urging it on a little. The warrior Bharata must have been quite amazed to learn that everything is in the Vedas, that they existed even before the universe and that Brahma, by reciting them, created the world. Let us not laugh too much, we almost fell into the same exaggerations in connection with the Bible and we escaped from them just in time.

Suffering, the fruit of maya and of action, is an ineluctable consequence of the human condition: "Everything is suffering for the wise
man," says Patannjali (Yogasutras, 11, 15). "Even pleasure is
suffering, because it is followed by suffering" writes Anindha, com-
menting on the Samkhya Sutra.

Once this notion of universal suffering was established, the philosophers of India sought either to escape from it or deny it. Let us again
repeat, man cannot resign himself to an antihuman situation, *he is not
free* to adhere to any deadly theory, while continuing to live. So
Samkhya and Yoga deny suffering as such, because it does not affect
the immortal and impassive Self: Since sorrows, volitions, thoughts
are not really us. The supreme Self has never been subjected, it is
free in all eternity, since it has relations only with itself. But, as
Eliade observes, if the *Parusa* is perfectly pure and static, why does it
allow becoming, experience and sorrow? Here the Hindus answer
that things are as they are and it is necessary to make the best of them
without inquiring too closely into their reason for being. A curious
answer, which would hardly please a Westerner and with which they
themselves are not too satisfied. Buddha thought to find the solution
by completely dissolving the soul-spirit insofar as it is individual and
by replacing it by unsubstantial acts of consciousness whose aggrega-
tion in a "me" is only an illusion. The Vedanta is satisfied to deny
the universe, which is maya.

Former lives

But punishment, karma, accumulated by every bad act—and which
every good action causes to decrease—must be exhausted. It is a very
prolonged task and a whole life would not suffice for it. Hence it will
be necessary to be born a thousand or a hundred thousand times, until
the stored-up karma is exhausted and final liberation is achieved.
Therefore another Hindu characteristic is the notion of multiple lives
anterior and posterior to present existence. The Hindus think that
certain yogis who achieve a complete mastery of their techniques can
recall them. I believe that psychic investigations have been pushed
very far in India and that Yoga perhaps permits access to a kind of

general undifferentiated consciousness, as if recollections clung to the world itself after the disappearance of the body. Which does not necessarily prove the existence of anterior lives or reincarnation.

The gods incarnate themselves as often as it is necessary in order to help mankind. "The only god plunges into the Ocean of life, incarnates himself, and calls himself Krishna. He plunges another time and emerges at another place in mankind and calls himself Jesus" (Ramakrishna). Liberated souls accompany God and also take on a new body, without having consciousness in general. Ramakrishna believed he could recognize six of these souls around him: One, Brahmanda, had been the soul of a playmate of Krishna, two others, Ramakrishnanda and Saraoanda, disciples of Jesus; and Balaram Bose, disciple of Chaitanya. He added that many of Christ's companions, as well as Joseph and John the Baptist were probably in this situation.

Among this flowering of gods, images of the Only One and of which there exist several millions in India, each one—according to the Hindus themselves—picks the personal divinity (*ishta devata*) which suits him best. For many roads lead to the same place, even if they seem to go in an opposite direction. This is a characteristic approach of Hindu thought, whose frenzied desire for synthesis often neglects evidence and even common sense.

Liberation

How do they arrive at this liberation from rebirths? By means of the total exhaustion of the stored-up karma. It can be achieved by short cuts which unfortunately few men follow to the end. First of all it is necessary, a condition *sine qua non*, to withdraw from the world. This is why the dream of many Hindus is to end their lives as an ascetic wandering in solitude and nourished only by alms.

It will then be necessary, without ever ceasing to practice all kinds of austerities, to choose a Yoga (a yoke), a discipline which leads to knowledge as the ultimate fruit. Another characteristic trait is the enormous importance which the Hindus attach to the *techniques* of asceticism, to the Yogas. These are of several kinds: They more particularly concern the physique (hatha yoga), the intelligence (jnana yoga), the affective life (bhakti yoga), etc. But Eliade has written such beautiful pages on this that one has misgivings in dealing with them after him. Let us say simply that it is a question of becoming fully master of one's thoughts, of one's feelings, of one's will. But *one does not become their master except by extinguishing them,* in order to realize them as not being self; the recognition of the "me" and hence the supreme Self (for Brahma-Atman) is something else again. One of the familiar exercises of Yoga may perhaps make it easier to understand what it involves: this is the ekagrata (concentration on a single point). Thereby one concentrates on any object whatsoever, for example a chair or a door knob, and one measures the time during which one succeeds in not thinking about anything else. This time increases with exercise, but at the beginning the distracted mind seeks to run away "like the does in the garden of Benares," as the classic texts say. A very long repetition of this same exercise perfectly disciplines the attention with which one can then do as one wishes.

It is then that the much discussed *paranormal phenomena* appear, the "Siddhis" or "powers" according to the Indian vocabulary. The ascetic can stop his heart; this has been verified by Dr. Brosse with an electrocardiogram. Or, again, he can go into a state of hibernation with such a reduction of respiration exchanges that he can be buried for a very long time without it killing him.

These paranormal phenomena certainly exist, and Western science has verified a great number. Unquestionably this allows a favorable bias toward the existence of other even stranger Siddhis, recorded in the sacred books. So eminent an orientalist as Mircea Eliade has a very disquieting attitude toward them and seems to have acquired a very extensive personal experience of them. Perhaps the Hindus have realized the Bergsonian dream of a science of the mind whose objective—but not the methods—would very much differ from our Western science. They start out from an idea (that I believe proper and fruitful) of an almost unlimited power to train the mind and its functions, while Westerners barely train the body. One should be able to accomplish all kinds of acrobatics with his cerebral functions, perhaps by setting in motion these vast cortical zones which physiologists consider as untapped reserves. In his experiments Weiss has shown the almost absolute power of the attention and of the will over nervous mechanisms: When as the result of serious accidents or war wounds, surgeons join the flexor nerve of the lower limbs to the extensor, the patient at first finds it impossible to coordinate his movements. But if *he attends to it* constantly, he will succeed at the end of a certain time and will be able to walk, *so long as he consciously wants to.* If his attention relaxes, he immediately falls. Thus, the order issued from the brain—and from the highest zones—can scorn anatomical barriers, chronaxia and the entire strangeness of the path, in order to arrive nevertheless at its aim.

Yet is it necessary to adopt all the conclusions that the Hindus draw from these experiments? No. It is fitting to screen with the methods of western science the incontestable results which they have attained, and which one will perhaps be able to interpret quite otherwise.

The last phases of liberation

The phase of the Siddhis must be gone beyond. Like the Christian mystic who is ashamed of his ecstasy and dissimulates as much as he can among his friends, all *gurus* forbid their adepts to show the Siddhis and above all to glory in them or to interest themselves in them: otherwise one would be a kind of acrobat incapable of supreme spiritual fulfillment. Further, and further, the mind detaches itself completely from the universe and the body, and the *samadhi* (the *satori* of the Japanese) occurs, a mysterious state from which one emerges no longer the same as one was upon entering it, and about which one can say nothing without having experienced it. The adept is no longer a man, he is a "jivanmukta," one "delivered while yet on earth," master of himself as of the universe. He has definitively abolished the cycle of rebirths; his acts, no matter what they are, no longer secrete karma. At the moment of his death, which he will determine at will, he will definitively disappear from the physical plane in order to merge himself with Brahma.

It seems very probable that some of these sublime jivanmuktas exist in India, even though they are lost amidst so many charlatans whose number and dishonesty the Hindus themselves deplore. But this so difficult liberation, which does not always reward the greatest sacrifices, is reserved only to a small number of elect. What then will the great mass of the human species do? Must it limit itself to acting passively, the least evilly that it can, without becoming capable of breaking the cycle of rebirths before numerous existences? The doctrine of the sages then becomes quite despairing and this undoubtedly is how too many Hindus understand it.

A very great mind, Aurobindo Ghose, who died not too long ago, advocates another path, practicable by the greatest number. Following the Hindu rule, he still sought for a means of salvation in the Scriptures. In the middle of the epic cycle of the Mahabharata, which relates the exploits and adventures of the first Aryans, the Bharatas, upon their arrival in India, there lies a pearl, the Bhagavad-Gita. In it Aurobindo has found the wherewithal to renew the "physique" of the act in his country. Certain orientalists do not admit his interpretations and think that he makes too great demands on the old text. Unquestionably, in fact, the West, which Aurobindo knew well, suggested to him—without his being aware of it—some ideas which were not at all so apparent in the Gita. But this does not mean to say that the philosopher of Pondichéry is completely in error. And the veritable devotion that the Hindus bring to the Bhagavad-Gita—for them it is what the *Imitation of Christ* is to a Catholic—proves that its cadenced strophes respond to a deep need of the Hindu soul and of the human soul in general.

The Bhagavad-Gita

At Kurukshetra the hero Arjuna, whose war chariot is being driven by the blue God Krishna, finds himself facing the immense army that he must fight. But, as the result of a whole series of vicissitudes and crimes, "Uncles and grandfathers, teachers, cousins, sons and grandsons, comrades, fathers-in-law, benefactors" confront each other in the opposite camps. Seeing this the hero despairs: It is not fear that makes his body tremble and his hair stand on end. But he suddenly realizes the cruelty of war. What good is it to besmirch oneself with the blood of his kin, even if they are the aggressors, even to reap the victory? "Even though they, blinded by greed, see no sin in destroying the family . . . why should we not have the wisdom to retreat before such a sin? It is better for me that the sons of Dhritarah- stra . . . massacre me disarmed and nonresistant." Having spoken thus, Arjuna sinks down in his chariot, the divine bow Gandiva, and the inexhaustible quiver slip far from his hands. Here he again finds the accent of other stanzas of the Mahabharata, those which the sweet Savitri addresses to Yama, the funeral god who carries off her husband's soul: "Do no violence to any being, neither in act, nor thought, nor word . . . this is the eternal law of the Just. This is what the world ordinarily does for those toward whom love inclines. But the good practice charity, even toward the enemy that fall into their hands."

Then Krishna comforts the "warrior of the powerful arm." First of all, the enemy "neither is born nor dies; he is not killed when the body is killed, but the incarnated soul sheds the old body and puts on a new one, just like a man exchanges a used garment for another." On the other hand *action is superior to inaction, on the condition of not concerning oneself with the fruits of the work.* When it must be carried out, when it constitutes a moral duty, it no longer gives place to karma, if the actor disregards the disappointment of failure as well as the joy of success—if he acts only with the Law in mind. In Arjuna's case the wicked deserved punishment, but he must apply it without hatred or excess: "Hence, arise and conquer glory, vanquish the enemy, and enjoy an opulent realm. For me and for nobody else they are already killed. Become merely the occasion . . ."

This is how the Gita exorcises the dangerous spell, so typically Hindu, of disgust with action. Good actions must be carried out. "The yoga of works is superior to the yoga of the renunciation of action . . . but you have a right to action, never to its fruits." Thus, even outside the sages of solitude, a practicable path opens up to the ordinary man. This is one of the heights of the Hindu system of motivation.

Resemblances to the Western motivational system

In his *The Perennial Philosophy*, Aldous Huxley, by juxtaposing passages of different origins, clearly showed the surprising kinship between Hindu and Christian mystics. Renunciation of the world,

renunciation of self, substitutions of the divine will for one's own—
we have known all that for the past two thousand years. Nor are we
ignorant of the notion of the act which involves consequences in this
world and the other. On reading the *Gita* we very often find ourselves
in a familiar country. Fortunately Huxley took care to recall the
origin of the passages cited in his book for otherwise at first sight it
would be difficult to distinguish St. John of the Cross from a passage
of the Chandogya or of the Brhadaranyaka Upanishad. I hardly
believe that one can explain everything by some relations between
the schools of the East and the West, except perhaps in the case of
Hesychasm, to be discussed in a moment. It seems more probable
to relate everything to the unity of human nature. When it gradually
raises itself toward its highest summits, it undoubtedly encounters
the same obstacles and it gets around them by the same means. The
spectacle which the adept, plunged in a terminal ecstasy, discovers
must be very close in all cases, even though the interpretation differs
(little enough) according to the philosophy peculiar to the time and
place.

The Christian Yoga

In general it is not realized that there once existed Christian yogis:
these were the hesychast mystics of Mount Athos (esuxia, peace,
appeasement) who lived during the first centuries of our millennium.

Their school flourished between the eleventh and fourteenth centuries on Mount Athos. Like the yogis they had noticed that all
psychic activity involves a somatic repercussion; whence arose the
idea of doing things in reverse, i.e., inducing the loftiest meditations
by an appropriate somatic technique. The deeper study of this
psycho-physiological discovery—since it is such, and I believe that
we barely see its first consequences—led them to distinguish, as in
India, a certain number of "centers" (the cerebro-frontal center, the
oro-laryngeal center, the pectoral center, the cardiac center) which
have nothing physiologically definite about them. The ascetic simply
observed that by concentrating on these zones the attention produces
different effects. The hesychasts insisted especially on concentration
on the "cardiac center, the place of the heart," and gave numerous

technical details on the method of psycho-physiological prayer: "Then," says Gregory Palamas "sit thee down on a low chair, let thy intelligence descend from thy head to thy heart and keep it there in this place; then, bending forward as much as thou canst until thou feelst a keen pain in thy chest, thy muscles and neck, then cry out with thy heart and soul, 'Lord Jesus Christ, have pity on me!' . . . By holding thy breath as long as thou canst, by relegating thy mind to thy heart and by patiently multiplying thy appeals to Lord Jesus, thou wilst rapidly break and annihilate thoughts of every order, even good ones."

According to Simeon the New Theologian the following must be done: "When thou art alone in thy cell shut thy door, and seat thyself in a corner; raise thy mind, above all things vain and transient; recline thy beard and chin on thy breast, turn thy eyes and thy thought towards the middle of thy belly, the region of the navel and search the place of the heart, the seat of the soul. At first all will be dark and comfortless but if thou perserverest day and night, thou wilt find an ineffable joy; and no sooner has the soul discovered the place of the heart than it is involved in a mystic and ethereal light . . ."

Nicephorus the Abstainer advised those who were not able to find "the place of the heart" by the previous technique to repeat ceaselessly the "Prayer of Jesus," in a deliberate mechanical manner. It is very exactly like the continuous recitation of the Mantra on which certain *Tantra* techniques in India insist so much.

Are we in the presence of a body of original discoveries, or was there a direct influence from Hindu ascetics? Without making claim to a particular competence in the matter, I confess that I would incline more toward the first hypothesis. Obviously there was no lack of contacts between India and Greece ever since Alexander the Great, and the philosophers of Hellas had been struck by the theories and behavior of the Hindu gymnosophists. But one finds such a particular language in the instructions of the monks of Mount Athos. The "centers" are described in so characteristic a manner, even though several of them may be superimposed on homologous centers in yoga. Finally, one finds so few typically Hindu allusions or reminiscences in Athos, that I am led to believe in an independent discovery rather than in a transmission.

But hesychasm—and this is a very interesting phenomenon—had only a relatively brief life. It seems that Christians were a little shocked by the technical aspect of the gymnastic breathing exercises and their relation to the quest for divinity. They very quickly preferred the way which Hindus call bhakti yoga or jnana yoga (the yoga of devotion and the mind), or more exactly a middle way which partakes of the two. Let us note moreover, for the sake of objectivity, that the Hindus know perfectly well that one can short-circuit the arduous techniques of the Hatha yoga and arrive at a definitive liberation through bhakti or jnana yoga.

The differences

But it would be a serious illusion to make overhasty conclusions on the basis of these undeniable similarities. Because there are also differences, which may appear subtle, but which involve consequences of capital importance.

First, for us Christians *the world is not maya, and it is not bad.* Perhaps one will find the first affirmation of the good present in the creation from the very first chapter of Genesis. God separates the light from the darkness; he forms the great luminous bodies which will preside over day and night, he commands the waters to bring forth the creeping creatures having life, and the earth to produce plants which will bear seed, each according to its kind. And to conclude, he creates man, "To the image of God he created him: male and female he created them." The phrase "And God saw that it was good" is repeated in Genesis like a leitmotif. Now, if in the Vedas one finds expressions of wonderment before the splendors of the universe (I have given an example), the gaze of the sages were to turn away from the vision in the Upanishads in order to consider the means of escaping from it.

The evolution of ideas was not so simple among the Christians and among them, I believe, one can find a double current. Undoubtedly the first comes to us from certain passages of the Gospel in which Christ curses the world; in truth, this would be the world of the wicked and the Pharisees, for it would be absurd for the Creator to curse his creation. Later, the fathers of the desert, who lived a furious asceticism in the Thebaid, were to magnify certain maledictions, sometimes to excess, by taking them out of context. St. Anthony (who suffered from sexual impotence, if one is to believe a recent study which is, however, contestable) valued marriage only insofar as "it can serve to procreate virgins." Later, St. Bernard was to close his eyes upon passing a charming landscape which might risk turning him away from contemplation of the One God. The *Imitation* was to hail the ascetic who separates himself completely from the world:

"Why do you wish to see what is not lawful for you to have? The world passes away and the concupiscence thereof. The sensual appetite entices you to go abroad, but when the hour is past, what do you bring back with you but remorse of conscience and a heavy heart? A merry going forth often leads to a sad return, and a glad eventide a mournful dawn" (i. 20).

But in numerous passages, it is very clear that it is the world of men and its vain agitation which is the target, and not at all the work of God in nature.

This work of God has always been celebrated by a second current of thought, already very apparent in the Old Testament. We have seen that it is formally declared good, with a great insistence, in the very first sentences of Genesis. Later, the sacred cantors were never to forget either its grandeur or mystery. Yahveh speaks to Job to ask him:

"Where were you when I founded the earth? ... Who has stretched the measuring line for it? ... Have you entered the storehouse of the snow, and seen the treasury of the hail? ... Have you fitted a curb to the Pleiades? Can you bring forth the Mazzaroth in their season or guide the Bear with its train?"

The Psalmist celebrates the works of God in Psalm 103:

"How manifold are your works, O Lord! In wisdom you have wrought them all—the earth is full of your creatures;

"The sea also, great and wide, in which are schools without number of living things both small and great....

"They all look to you to give them food in due time.

"When you give it to them, they gather it; when you open your hand, they are filled with good things.

"If you hide your face, they are dismayed; if you take away their breath, they perish and return to their dust.

"When you send forth your spirit, they are created, and you renew the face of the earth."

Finally, Psalm 148, is animated by a spirit of the same order as that of the singer of the Arthavaveda. But here, Yahveh is always present behind the marvels of the earth:

"Praise the Lord from the heavens, praise him in the heights. . . .

"Praise him, sun and moon; praise him all you shining stars.

"Praise him you highest heavens. . . .

"Praise the Lord from the earth, you sea monsters and all depths;

"Fire and hail, snow and mist, storm winds that fulfill his word;

"You mountains and all you hills, you fruit trees and all you cedars;

"You wild beasts and all tame animals, you creeping things and you winged fowl.

"Let the kings of the earth and all peoples, the princes and all the judges of the earth,

"Praise the name of the Lord, for his name alone is exalted."

This beauty, this goodness of the work of God, permeates the mind and the heart of the Christian people. Perhaps, in passing, we shall see in this one of the causes of the ferocious repression of the Albigensians. Obviously, the barons of the North were delighted to be able to be agreeable to God by looting the chateaux of their colleagues in the South, and their motives had nothing very pure about them. But the sacred horror in the face of a doctrine which declared the universe of the Only God bad certainly constituted a not so negligible factor in their conduct.

This idea that the universe is good, and even as good as it possibly can be in the circumstances in which God had willed it, was to be taken up by all the theologians, and joined it to that of its profound adaptation to man, king of creation. Thus, it is not only beautiful and good, but even more sovereignly worthy of interest and study, since it serves to exalt divine glory. Obviously, these same theologians were not ever to forget the other face, the Other World, the true fatherland of man, infinitely more beautiful and more desirable than the one here below. This is a characteristic approach of Christianity, a crucial zone on which we can never dwell too much: here it retains seemingly contradictory aspects of reality; it refuses to reject the one or the other; it proclaims the existence of a link between them, hidden provisionally, or in certain cases, definitively, from our intelligence.

We see it in the conception of the world—excellent and worthy of praise—yet there exists another one infinitely more desirable. In the idea of evil, a negative reality—and yet God is sovereignly good. In the idea of human freedom, which one cannot deny, and on which everything rests—yet God knows everything in advance (because for him doubtlessly, time does not exist). And better still, perhaps, we see this in the so singular dogma of the *resurrection of the body* on the last day. The body must be humbled, it must be mortified in order to become a docile instrument of the spirit. And yet it constitutes an admirable mechanism assembled by the Creator. It will be reconstituted at the end of the world. God will not judge only souls, but souls in their bodies.

Thus a problem, a tension is created in the intelligence. *It is this tension which creates science.* Undoubtedly the Greeks arrived at an explanation of the universe by other ways. But Christianity supported with its immense authority two essential concepts:

a) The world has a meaning, since it is the work of a sovereignly intelligent God.

b) This meaning is adapted to man and renders the universe worthy of interest, since it is the work of a sovereignly good God.

The explanation is not given in advance, as in the Vedas which obtained it only "by throwing out the baby with the bath water." We have only general directions along which we must work, in order to solve temporary contradictions. It is not by chance that science, while born in Greece, has developed only in Christendom. And if in the Middle Ages we almost did take the "oriental turn," of which De Rougemont speaks, we caught ourselves very quickly. We did not reduce all activity of the Christian to the close scrutiny of the Book of books.

The physics of action in Christendom

We also believe that every act involves its good or bad consequences, *but we do not need multiple existences in order to exhaust the karma in them.* Each second of this earth is accorded to us but once, it will have infinite consequences as a result, and its importance, as I have already said, is without parallel. And on the other hand, the consequences of the act *are not fatal in an absolute sense.* The greatest of sinners, let us repeat, can be saved at the last moment of his free destiny, by an act of love of God and of completely disinterested repentance. And the most simple action, offered to God with a pure heart, is refracted through the merits of Jesus and the communion of saints, it unleashes infinite mechanisms and subtle compensations, and can save an estranged soul already more than three-quarters lost. This is perhaps the most important difference with the religion of Brahma: *the karmic addition and subtraction are not automatic,* since the merits of Jesus and the goodness of God come between the act and the adding machine. A single perfectly good act (that is to say, according to Hindu and Christian criteria) turned entirely toward God, and from which all idea of personal reward is excluded, can always save everything, up to the last dying breath. The Christian does not know the terrible Wheel, the obsession of India, precisely because *his God is not confused with a law of nature* and is *personal* (granting immediately that the term "personal" is only a rough approximation). Everything can be paid, and paid in an instant. Everybody can do everything always, for himself and above all for others.

The Christian religion: doctrines of action and solidarity. Hindu religions: techniques of individual liberation, in which however some ascetics consent to aid their brothers "out of pity for the world." Moreover the Hindu has naught else before his eyes but a cold and inexplorable law, and no other concern but to escape it. The Christian yearns for his God who has made everything and who still does everything for him at every moment. In the second case the stimulus seems more powerful, the efficaciousness in the moral life greater, and the degree of truth higher.

Action is king in Christendom. It is already written in the Gospel: "Not everyone who says to me, 'Lord, Lord,' shall enter the kingdom of heaven; but he who does the will of my Father in heaven shall enter the kingdom of heaven." And the *Imitation* pursues this idea: "For it is not learning that makes a man holy and just, but a good life makes him pleasing to God. . . . A humble rustic that serves God is more acceptable to him than is a proud intellectual who neglects his soul to study the course of the heavens." (i. 1-2). It is not enough to think, to pray; one must also act. "If you are lost in ecstasy," writes a great mystic, "and a poor man comes to ask you for a bowl of soup, leave your ecstasy there and go heat the soup!" Here we find ourselves before another fundamental motif of the West. And even if its origins are forgotten, their effects continue to make themselves felt.

Oneself and others

The concept of charity and love of one's neighbor is very well known and practiced in India (see the stanzas of the Savatri *above*). But personal liberation remains the most important thing. The hero is the ascetic in the forest. Now in the Gospel there is a precept that is repeated many times with an insistence of which the Upanishads give no example; it is, "Love one another." This notion of the welfare of others, of the neighbor that one must love as oneself, of the kingdom of God to which one does not gain access all alone but along with others, is one of the essential features of Christianity. A mysterious feature, moreover, if it is considered deeply: Why this insistence on the group, as if it were necessary that the whole species progress, and not just the individual? Or rather does this insistence on "the others" hide a particular characteristic of human nature, perhaps some subtle links which we do not discern—or discern not yet?

Conclusion

This too rapid analysis hardly touches the subject, but it is sufficient to the determination of our attitude or the confirmation thereof. We bow respectfully before the long-haired ascetic, the *muni* of the wild desert. We properly appreciate the heroic efforts which bring him close to the One. What he sees, our saints have seen, just as well or even better. But we shall not exchange the message of Christ for his. For a subtle poison mixes with the most magnificent stanzas of the Upanishads, which makes the whole motivation toxic. Disgust with the universe, the aloofness from acts, thirst for liberation from the intolerable burden of life, does this not explain the masses of India, dying of hunger without engaging in a struggle against harsh nature? This degradation, this cowardice, cannot belong to the Way; rather they flow from a theory that has grasped only *a part* of human motivations.

What the sage of Rishikesh, or the *Sadhus* of their remote ashramas possess, we have too. But we hold something more, a more complete truth. And it is not by chance that evolution resumed its rapid march only in Christendom—and there alone.

6

Conversion: The Technique of Communication

The mind is rid of intellectualist prejudices which barred the path of religious experience to it. It acknowledges the interest of the phenomenon, and the history of religions has instructed it about its generality, its intensity and several of its broadest characteristics. The mind is likewise acquainted with the mechanism of the two principal religions of humanity. Christianity, the religion of its fathers, is now better known to it, taking account of its deviations in history, and of the poor way it has often been presented.

Even more, the mind would like to believe, because it knows that it lacks the indispensable springs of motivation. But it does not believe, that is to say, it does not realize the relation between an abstract conviction and a rule of life. How does one divert the intellect into the river of action? So, the mind wishes and does not wish; it does not understand what holds it back and it despairs.

This involves a banal difficulty which undoubtedly stems from the very nature of this motivation which we so poorly understand. But let us remain faithful to the method we have been using, that is, let us avoid speculation as much as possible before having consulted observation.

The study of conversion by the observation of converts

The time is passed when different authors like de Sanctis and Harms could consecrate studies to converts which were quite honest, but inspired a bit too much by a summary Freudianism. As in many other areas, concrete observation here teaches us that reality hardly fits into the carcan of ambitious theories and hasty conclusions. Things are more complex, and it is necessary to refer to monographs and clinical observations of converts. These studies have already passed the beginning phase. They constitute an interesting chapter of religious psychology. And, as was to be expected, they have disclosed a series of particularities to which sufficient attention had not been paid. Because of a lack of documentation from other religions, I shall here consider only conversions to Roman Catholicism. Naturally, it is not my aim to write a complete treatise, but, as in the preceding chapters, only to sift out the principal characteristics of the phenomenon. The best thing to do, it seems to me, is to discuss in the form of "clinical notes"—summarized as much as possible—a certain number of cases where precise information is available. One can already distinguish roughly between conversions of a "progressive" and a "catastrophic" type.

The "progressive" conversion

In the *progressive type*, I would include Psichari, Gertrude von Le Fort, Charles Nicolle, Jacques Rivière, etc. Here, faith was lost very early in life, or it never existed. It was found again after long investigations and meditations interspersed with more or less long periods in which the interest in religious problems diminished or disappeared. The return to God and the restoration of religious practice took place at the end of a number of years. Either these people were particularly reserved (it does not seem so), or else the return to faith was effected progressively, passing along paths that were chiefly intellectual. But here, as we know, we must accord the word "intellect" a very broad meaning. Such processes do not pose special problems. Much more widespread are the sudden accidents, with "illuminations" which strongly impress—and most of the time definitively—the person who experiences them.

The "catastrophic" conversion

We shall now discuss a certain number of cases of this type, all of which exhibit a "family resemblance."

PAUL CLAUDEL

Antecedents: Indifferent family; around the age of 18, he adhered to a monist materialism; made his first communion; seems to have preserved a terrible recollection of his years as an unbeliever. Haunted by the idea of death.

The phenomenon: A short time before, he had been saddened by the deaths of his grandfather and of a granduncle, whose agony had been very painful. He was likewise struck, in an imprecise way, by reading Rimbaud. Several months later, he sought in the ceremonies of the Church a stimulus for writing. He went to high Mass; nothing special occurred. He returned for Vespers. In an instant, he says, his heart was touched and he believed, while listening to a hymn which he was told later was the "Magnificat." "A heart-rending feeling of the innocence and the eternal childhood of God. . . . How happy are the people who believe! . . . if it is nevertheless true? It is true! God exists and he is there. He is someone, he is a being as personal as myself. He loves me, he calls me . . ." Claudel began to cry on hearing the hymn, "Adeste, fideles" sung with a magnificent tenderness.

The consequences: No immediate ones. Four years of struggles and hesitations at the end of which he made his confession and definitively changed his life.

ALEXIS CARREL

Antecedents: Studied the humanities with the Jesuits. Lost his faith after studying medicine for several years. Came to the conviction that no certainty is valid outside the scientific fact (but he obviously also restricted the very definition of scientific fact). Dissatisfied, he feels a torment in the depths of himself.

The phenomenon: It involves the famous story of Marie Ferrand (Marie Bailly). Carrel was accompanying the sick in the train bound for Lourdes. His attention concentrated on Marie Bailly: tubercular peritonitis in its final stage. He made his observation on the night before arrival, he tried to calm her sufferings and said to himself, "If she recovers, I shall believe." At Lourdes Marie Bailly entered into her death agony. Carrel opposed immersing her in the pool. She was merely sprinkled lightly with water, then, dying, she was carried on a cot before the grotto.

Suddenly at 2:40 (Carrel noted the hour), the young girl's features took on color, her pulse recovered, her stomach lost its swelling. Carrel did not believe his eyes. At 3 o'clock Marie asked for a glass of milk and declared herself cured.

The consequences: Carrel was to take many years before he was to fully realize his conversion, above all because he confused the dogmas with hypotheses or theories to which Catholics are in no wise forced to adhere. In 1943 his conversion was complete, and he died as a Christian.

CHARLES DE FOUCAULD

Antecedents: Very dissolute youth. Much more preoccupied with women, gambling and good wines rather than with the holy Church. During the course of a tour of duty south of Oran, he followed his regiment with much courage and abnegation; then he undertook his famous exploration of Morocco. Very impressed by the religion of the Jews and Arabs which did not defer to public opinion. He sought his path in living with rectitude, work and prayer, but *he did not himself believe.* He asked God, if he existed, to show himself.

The phenomenon: One day he went into abbe Huvelin's confessional and asked the abbé to enlighten him on the Catholic religion. The abbé replied, "Confess yourself and you will believe." Foucauld did so, almost under compulsion, and the abbé made him take communion immediately.

The consequences: A total and brutal conversion, in the sense of the word *convertere.* He immediately entered the Trappe of Notre-Dame des Neiges, and then the Trappe of Akbes in Syria. He was to become the hermit of the Sahara.

ADOLPHE RETTE, *A very typical case.*

Antecedents: Raised by a frenziedly anticlerical grandfather. Pursued very whimsical studies. Failing in business, he enlisted with the 12th Cuirassiers. He was happy in this unit. Then he flirted with the symbolist poets, led a very dissolute life. Married a very Christian girl in a civil ceremony (no religious marriage). His wife died. Very anticlerical and very sensual in his writings.

The phenomenon: One evening in Fontainebleau he was speaking before a small audience, announcing the arrival of the Golden Age.

But when some persons in the audience questioned him, he was forced to acknowledge the lacunae in science. A heretofore unknown malaise then came over him and *astonished* him. "A remorse and at the same time an unutterable joy" shook him completely. But immediately afterwards, a violent impulse drove him in an opposite direction, and he wrote a virulent article against the Church. He tore it up during the night. On the next day he went into the forest, reflected for a long time, knelt down and prayed. His soul flowered, and from this moment on he believed in God. But he did not dare present himself to a priest. One night, a violent impulse led him almost to commit suicide. He clutched his bed in order not to give into it, while calling upon God for help. Then he heard ("I heard it, yes, I heard it, I swear it on my eternal salvation!") a voice tell him that God was there, and the impulse disappeared.

The consequences: He went to see a priest, converted completely and became a veritable lay apostle.

Leon Bloy, *"The Ungrateful Beggar"*

Antecedents: Voltairian father, Catholic mother. First Communion, during which he did not understand a thing, guided by "functionary" priests who acquitted themselves mechanically of their tasks. Obviously, he lost his faith. A youth of failure; very sad. He met Barbey d'Aurevilly whose seigniorial air subjugated him. Contact with the latter made him aware of the slight basis of certain of his prejudices against religion. Long tergiversations.

The phenomenon: It was in 1869, on the day of the Feast of St. Peter, that he made his confession, and re-entered the Church. The phenomenon seems to have been very violent, even though he was reserved about the circumstances surrounding it. "He had been seized by the throat by someone stronger than he; his soul had been snatched . . . then he was thrown head first into an old confessional whose planks creaked under his weight . . . And all this had been carried out in the same instant."

The consequences: An ardent neophyte. Tempted by the monastic life, he desired to become a Benedictine. But, seven years after his conversion, he entered into a state of concubinage with a prostitute from whom he could not succeed in separating himself, despite two flights to the Trappists. Then the poor girl became a fervent Christian, she meditated on the Gospel, believed she had revelations and ended up by going mad. Bloy took refuge in La Grande Chartreuse, but the monks dissuaded him from a contemplative life. Shortly afterward he married Jeanne Molbech, a young Danish girl whom he had converted. Admirable home life, very poor.

George Devallieres

Antecedents: Father an unbeliever, mother pious and devout. First Communion at which he understood nothing. At fifteen he broke with the faith completely. A disordered life; but he felt pity and tenderness in the face of misery. He read *Là-bas* and *En route* by Huysmans; he met Bloy, whom he admired. Preserved a certain veneration for the Blessed Virgin.

The phenomenon: In Notre-Dame-des-Victoires, a church which he knew well, he saw a very slovenly priest go by. Suddenly it seemed to him that a voice spoke imperiously to him, " 'That's enough. . . . Go recite the Credo, there, your forehead against the stone'." I went there, and then I told myself later, You have only to make your confession." (He went into the first confessional he saw) "And I said to myself, providing it is not this slob, this disgusting priest. . . . But it turned out to be just he. The confession did me an immense good."

The consequences: He began to paint his celebrated Sacré-Coeur. Complete conversion with no reservations.

Manuel Garcia Morente, Spanish philosopher (1882-1942).

Antecedents: Mother very pious, father very liberal. He lost his faith, or what little he had of it, around twenty, on coming to France to study. A part of his family was massacred during the Spanish Civil War. He succeeded in returning to France just in time. He had been struck by a visit to Ligugé several years before.

The phenomenon: One night, after his return to France; Paris, 2 o'clock in the morning. He had been disturbed all day about his family from whom he had received no news. Then he heard a concert of French music over the radio. His eyes filled with tears on hearing Berlioz's *Enfance de Jésus;* he thought of his own pious childhood, of Jesus the child, Jesus forgiving, Jesus on the cross followed by a crowd which rises toward him. Morente saw himself among this crowd, riveted to the ground, unable to move. He fell to his knees, and tried to say the Our Father which he had forgotten. An immense peace came over his soul. He fell asleep in front of the window for a moment. Suddenly he woke up and felt that Christ was there. "He was there. . . . I did not see him, I did not hear him, I did not touch him. . . . But he was there. . . ." This "perception without sensation" of the visit of the Lord lasted more than an hour.

The consequences: His real conversion was delayed for more than a year. Then he took holy orders and exercised a great influence as a priest and philosopher.

Kenyon Reynolds

Antecedents: Eminent American industrialist, one of the founders of the Standard Oil Company. Typically American in his behavior. Pious Protestant childhood. Good and pious father. Having acquired an enormous fortune, he retired from business very early, declaring that he was no longer interested in making money (which astonished his compatriots). He married a young Catholic girl. Then came the death of his brother, Graham, a Catholic priest. It was only after this death that he became interested in the Catholic religion and informed himself about it from its ministers. Seven years of hesitations.

The phenomenon: One day in San Francisco, he looked at the city and thought about the sentence, "Thou hast the words of eternal life . . . And we have believed and have known, that thou art Christ, the son of God." He wished to believe and asked God to send him the Spirit which vivifies. His heart was suddenly inundated by the joy of the divine presence and the peace of certitude.

The consequences: He entered the Catholic Church several months later. His wife died after a few years and he became a Benedictine.

Max Jacob, an extreme case.

Antecedents: Of a Jewish family of Quimper. During his childhood he was forbidden to go into Catholic Churches which interested him nevertheless. In 1900, he went to Paris and achieved fame as a poet after some disappointments. Very gay in society and appreciated for his clownish jokes. Attracted by the occult sciences. Very disordered life. He often thought about suicide, despite his successes.

The phenomenon: Very brutal, hallucinatory behavior. On September 7, 1909, he came back from the Bibliothèque Nationale. "I put down my portfolio, I looked for my bedroom slippers, and when I raised my head there was Someone on the wall . . . What beauty, what elegance, what sweetness . . . His shoulders . . ., His bearing . . ., He was wearing a robe of yellow silk and blue ornaments. He turned around, and I saw this peaceful and radiant face . . ."

The consequences: A change of behavior. He was never to forget his vision, but he hesitated five years, tossed between different tendencies. He never ceased to pray, was always very charitable, but his life was still disordered. One evening, a little Jewish hunchback, whom he did not know and to whom he expressed his desire to be baptized, told him about the Fathers of Zion who concern themselves with the conversion of the Jews. He went there immediately, but the instruction was long and hard, and demanded a reform of his ways.

Then a *second phenomenon* as brutal as the first: he saw Christ at the cinema, on the screen. Overcome, he recounted his vision but he was made fun of and his baptism was retarded. In order to console himself he made daily visits to the Sacré-Cœur in Montmartre. He was finally baptized, but did not succeed in living a more chaste life. It was then that he was hit by an auto. He was taken to a hospital, where he was vividly struck by the idea of death. He then fled to Paris and retired to Saint-Benoît-sur-Loire where he prayed and led an austere life, occasionally marked by lapses.

EDITH STEIN (1891–1943)

Antecedents: Celebrated German philosopher, pupil of Husserl. Very orthodox Jewish family. She very much admired her mother, who seems to have been a superior woman. Philosophy gradually detached her from any belief in a personal God. Nevertheless now and again the search for God allured her.

The phenomenon: Sudden aspect. In 1921 she spent her vacation in the Bavarian countryside and came upon the life of St. Teresa. She read it to the end without being able to tear herself away from it, nor interrupt her reading, throughout the entire night. "As I closed the book, I said to myself, 'This is the truth'." That very morning she went to buy a catechism and a Missal, then after having studied them she went to Mass and had herself baptized.

The consequences: She gave up her teaching duties at the University of Freiburg and in part the reputation as a philosopher. She spent long hours in prayer among the nuns and discovered her monastic vocation. She became a Carmelite nun in 1933 and wrote her great work "Infinite Being and the Eternal God," an exposition of philosophy from Descartes to Heidegger, in the Carmelite convent. She was deported by Hitler as a Jew and died in Ausschwitz.

JACQUES AND RAISSA MARITAIN

Antecedents: Both were haunted by metaphysical problems. Raïssa, who came from a Russian Jewish family which had emigrated to Paris, lost her faith at sixteen, despite her efforts to hold on to it. At the Sorbonne (!) she sought for what "I needed to justify existence. . . . That which seemed to me necessary in order that life be not a thing sinister and useless." Maritain was born in a mixed Protestant-Catholic family. At sixteen, when he was a philosophy student at Henri IV, "he rolled in desperation on the floor of his room because he had no answers to all his questions."

One day Jacques and Raïssa were walking together in the Jardin des Plantes, and after desperately making an inventory of their conclusions, they decided to commit suicide if life did not disclose its true meaning to them before too long.

The phenomenon: It had an intellectual aspect with these two intensified "cerebralists." They attended Bergson's lectures during which he explained the "Enneads" of the Neo-Platonic mystic Plotinus to a very small class. It was a veritable illumination. One evening Raïssa, upon re-reading the passage in Plotinus on the relations between God and the soul, knelt before the book and covered it with kisses. She also read Pascal and Ruysbrœck. She married Maritain in 1904. It was later that they met Léon Bloy, after having read some of his works which made a very strong impression on them. But they hesitated very much because it seemed to them that in order to adhere to Christianity, they would have to abandon philosophy. They spent eight terrible months after an illness afflicted Raïssa, who seemed once or twice to have experienced typical phenomena: "Once in my sleep I heard these words which were said to me with a certain impatience:

You are always looking for what is to be done, there is nothing else but to love God and to serve him with all your heart." "Later," reported Raïssa, "I found these words in the *Imitation* which I had not yet read."

The consequences: Finally there was a definitive conversion. Then the Maritains exerted that influence in Catholic circles, familiar to all.

The Maritains were the beginning of a series from which I shall still take some examples. The "phenomena" there are less clear, less positive, more spread out in time. They disclose an intellectual comprehension, more or less strongly tinged with affectivity.

THOMAS MERTON

Mother a Quaker; father, vaguely religious, a painter. Only the rudiments of religion; no systematic religious training. He adhered to Anglicanism. During a trip to Rome, he was deeply struck by the art in the churches, especially on visiting Sts. Cosmas and Damian. For the first time in his life, he asked himself with astonishment "Who is the person men call Christ?" He bought a copy of the New Testament, he read it with pleasure, then continued to visit the churches, moved by an interest which was not only artistic. One evening he had an almost physical feeling of the presence of his dead father whom he had loved very much. At the same time he felt the misery of his moral situation. "And now I think for the first time in my whole life I really began to pray . . . out of the very roots of my being." On the next day he climbed to Santa Sabina, his soul full of contrition. He got on his knees and said the Pater. Afterwards he left Rome, went to England and forgot all this. He took some courses and interested himself a little in politics. One day he opened Gilson's book on medieval philosophy and understood "that the belief of Catholics was by no means the vague and rather superstitious hangover from an unscientific age. . . . On the contrary, here was a notion of God that was at the same time deep, precise, simple and accurate." This time the character of his life changed. He began to read the *Imitation*.

But he did not want to go to Mass. Then he began to hear an inner voice urging him sweetly, gently and strongly, "Go to Mass! Go to Mass!" Very moved, he entered a church and heard a sermon which did him some good. One September day, upon reading Newman's letters, he once again heard the inner voice, say to him, "What are you waiting for . . ., Why are you sitting here? . . . You know what you ought to do? Why don't you do it?" He went out in the rain and ran to the church asking for baptism.

Then, he again became very lukewarm, he resumed his literary life and did not really pray. Finally, while with a group of friends, a deep movement of his consciousness clearly showed Thomas Merton that he was to become a priest. And he entered the Trappist Order in which he remained after many struggles. He has written poems and essays which are very well known in Anglo-American reading audiences.

The VAN DER MEERS

A Dutch artist couple. They began by becoming enamored of a humanitarian socialism full of generosity. Then they came to Paris, frequenting artistic circles of which they very quickly grew tired. They were agnostics but nevertheless sought a solution to the problem of evil, suffering and inequality among men. A brief Nietzschean period. Very strong anti-Catholic prejudice.

During a visit to the Trappe at Westmalle, the chanting of the monks moved them very deeply. They were similarly affected by a visit to St. Peter's in Rome, struck by its grandiose character. Then they met Léon Bloy who pursuaded them to see a priest, and they converted to Catholicism. They noted that while discussing their conversion with the priest they hardly dared to voice their objections, so suddenly did these seem bereft of any force to them. After several days of anxiety, they received baptism. With the Van der Meers the phenomenon of an offensive reversion which is found among different converts may be observed: After a certain period of Christian life disgust, anxiety, a spiritual paralysis suddenly overwhelms the soul. "One is surrendered to an unknown force like in a bad dream." But it was only a trial, soon overcome.

J.-B. MAHN

Both his parents were painters, very close to each other; no religious education. Sometimes a grandmother took him to church, but this caused him only a certain sickness. After getting his degree in history, he specialized in monastic history and read the Gospel, in order to understand it fully. This had no special effect on him. He went to the Trappe at Scourmont in order to finish his doctoral thesis and was very impressed by the singing of "Salve, Regina." Père Maydieu invited him to the laying of the first cornerstone of the convent of Etiolles. "He felt a compulsion to kneel at the Elevation" and received baptism a year later.

KARL STERN

A German writer and biologist, he received a traditional Jewish education. Very intelligent (he knows it a little too well). Slightly sentimental, something of a poet. Hardly interested in the Catholic religion, until he met a fervent Christian, Frau Flamm, and a Japanese Christian family, the Yamagiwa. And also and above all, a poor servant Kati Huber, a true Christian who made a great impression on him. On the occasion of a talk given by Cardinal Faulhaber, Stern suddenly and for the first time saw "Judaism from the outside." But after this initial shock, his conversion was to require ten years of meditation, and it was to be necessary for him to meet Maritain, Dorothy Day and Père Couturier in order to complete it.

Let us conclude with an anonymous case described by Nédoncelle. The young man involved had a very estimable father, but who was systematically irreligious. Because religion had been presented to him very badly during his youth, it had seemed to him to be an obsession to be feared. All dogmas were ludicrous to him. For example, God delivers a man whom he calls his Son to executioners whom he created himself and invites a part of his creatures to come and praise him eternally for this exploit, in order to deliver the rest to eternal flames. Religion is a laughing stock and the child was quickly convinced. The idea that something real could exist in all this mumbo-jumbo hardly occurred to him. At eighteen, he was deeply stirred by one event: a friend was called to the colors (in 1915). He immediately realized that he could die and that death is the end of everything. The very object of the supreme sacrifice appeared absurd to him, for then the giving of one's all would be rewarded with nothingness. At this time he read the Gospel; but it did not seem "real" to him, because he had never thought of God as existing. On the other hand he was obsessed by the problem of evil: how to accept it? with suffering? He tried the philosophers and immediately saw all the holes in their assertions, which are quite apparent to a man coasting so near death, and seeing it present and inevitable. Later he became acquainted with some Catholics whom he found very engaging, and he suspected that his way of viewing religious problems was not the only one possible. He even began to pray but "that yielded nothing" and he soon stopped. But a very curious, and undoubtedly rare, thing happened. He resumed the study of the traditional proofs of the existence of God as formulated by Descartes, and in a short time found himself completely convinced.

The characteristics of the phenomenon of atheism

It would be extremely interesting to make an extensive review of the phenomenon of atheism in connection with this portrayal of conversions. Unfortunately this is hardly possible; there is still too little material assembled with the desirable scientific rigor. Gililand (1940) reported some observations made on 349 adolescent American students and found very few atheists among them. The majority were neutral or favorable to the idea of God and even toward the Church. Despite marked individual differences, there was scarcely any influence of their ideas on their behavior (see Chapter II on this subject). At the end of several years of university training, their ideas had hardly changed one way or other.

Much more important were Vetter's investigations among 600 members of the American Association for the Advancement of Atheism. Certain of his results illustrate the ignorance in which we still find ourselves on this subject. Some of the results are easily explainable, for example, the percentage of "intellectuals" interesting themselves in philosophical problems is clearly higher among atheists than it is among average Americans. The atheists are almost exclusively male. *The influence of parents is not such* as one might believe: for example, it is not at all evident that atheism is necessarily a family tradition. Among the parents of atheists, 82% belonged to a definite religion, and only 17% were free thinkers, agnostics or atheists. And among believing parents there were no proofs, on the contrary, that religion was weaker than the average; the atheists even tended to rate their parents as being more pious than average Americans are ordinarily. Very clearly there exists a *critical period* between the ages of fifteen and twenty, and this is the age when the immense majority of atheists declared that they had lost their faith (compared with the generally late age of conversion). The loss of faith can be slow and progressive or blunt, the two cases being found in an almost equal percentage. More than 75% of atheists *live in cities.* Many of them live in areas where their own beliefs are in the minority.

The causes attributed by the subjects for their atheism varied greatly: deepened knowledge of history and religion (cited by 75%): disgust with religious hypocrisy (60 times); influence of a book (55 times); influence of socialist materialism (30 times); effects of university education (25 times). Bereavements or death, the problem of evil, the horrors of war were more rarely mentioned. Nor was there either any relation with the precociousness of sexual experiences, which were divided in the same way among the nonatheists.

But other factors are more mysterious. For example *the premature death of parents:* 50% of the atheists who had lost all faith at the age of 20 had been orphaned (by one or both parents) before this date. Another, the rank of birth: for a long time it has been known that the psychology of the first-born child differs profoundly from that of his siblings. Now, 36% of the atheists were first-born, 15% younger children, and 9% only children. Thus atheism to a great measure depends on familial factors, the action of which seems quite obscure at present. Here we can only once more deplore the modest extent of our knowledge in the presence of problems of such great importance.

I have not found questionnaires dealing with the same subject in Europe that have the desirable scientific rigor. Those which I have read, and which dealt with the religion of intellectuals, were above all a pretext for making a show of high sounding phrases by those who were being interviewed. Thus the investigator who did not structure his questionnaire carefully enough, could not draw any valid findings from it. This is all the more unfortunate because there are good reasons to believe that the factors of disbelief among Europeans differ considerably from those among Americans.

It is also unfortunate that we are so poorly informed about the motivation substitutes of atheists: What do they substitute for God? And do they feel his absence, keenly or otherwise? On this capital subject, we have not yet emerged from the domain of personal impression.

Characteristics of the phenomenon of conversion

After this very abridged exposition of the several conversions on which we possess documentation, let us try to sift out the general features of the phenomenon.

Age seems to be an important factor. We can cite few conversions of very young people, undoubtedly because the great metaphysical questions are not *felt* before a certain age. As we have seen (Chap. II) death is a phenomenon completely devoid of reality to children and young people. It seems that the high tide of life must cease to rise and that the waters must slacken for man to begin to reflect on his life. Let us, however, not generalize too much. Missionaries report more than one conversion of very young people and even of children. But I think it involves another phenomenon different from that of the conversion of adults. The discursive processes are very much reduced, the authority of an adult, the attraction or admiration the young person feels for him are determinants. One does not see in evidence the "catastrophic processes" so frequent among adults. Everything seems much more gradual, because unquestionably there is hardly any resistance to overcome. This moreover does not diminish the solidity of the young person's convictions, as testified to by the numerous examples of martyrdom heroically borne by children (the martyrs of Uganda, for example). But among white adults of the twentieth century, the age of conversion is clearly situated between 40 and 60 years of age.

Sex does not seem to introduce very marked variations in the process. We do not have as many monographs on female conversions as we do on the male, but those which one can read do not indicate any very great differences in this matter. Except, perhaps, the greater violence of the affective process of the catastrophic type, which is habitually found in the female.

The *social milieu* has only an ambiguous role. Recent works have well established its importance in the Intelligence Quotient (IQ) which is regularly lower in the lower classes. And all verbal tests reveal a great inferiority in the *manipulation of language* among manual workers. Since this is the very bases of intellectual processes, it is probable that a little-developed intelligence corresponds to unpolished language. On the other hand unskilled laborers are not in the habit of writing their memoirs, nor do they submit voluntarily (at least in France) to inquiries about their religious development. This is so true that the picture of conversions is in danger of being distorted and just because of these factors. Finally, what percent of manual workers, deadened by long hours of purely material work, still find the courage, after a hard day, to reflect on the meaning of life? According to Nédoncelle, however, who reports only a few cases, there is not much difference in the phenomenon of conversion among the cultivated bourgeois and the workers. *But the process in itself* greatly varies according to individuals. Let us underline its curious catastrophic aspect breaking out after a more or less prolonged incubation. Earlier authors, like *de Sanctis* (1924) and Harms (1929), dwelt very much on the so-called "pathological" characteristics of the phenomenon, following the lines of Freudian thought. In their way of thinking, the converts are devoid of inner unity, their psyche is unstable. These people need to unify themselves, to shake off anxiety, and this is the hidden motivation of their story. Unable to remain alone, they invent a powerful Friend who completes them, comforts them and permits them to compensate perpetually for their failures. But the individual who has found peace of soul often loses his vitality. Humanly, a convert is a diminished personality.

These objections are simply absurd, and can be answered by a few general remarks. Nédoncelle first of all observes—and quite properly in my opinion—that causes in a human order would be the same within the hypothesis of conversion or in its opposite. The catastrophic phenomenon does not occur in every instance where previous behaviorial patterns would lend us to expect them. It is in no wise automatic. Moreover, what do these famous behaviorial patterns become when they are observed more closely? Their beautiful theoretical regularity vanishes. The history of the subjects before the "accident" is as varied as possible. Likewise it is with their social milieux, professions, characters, so far as we know them. As is

usually the case with a Freudian thesis, it is a brilliant but unde-
monstrable reconstruction, as I have said. One should have an
enormous mistrust of sciences in their infancy, like characterology
and psychiatry. The assurance of their votaries is directly proportional
to the fragility of their foundations. It is to be hoped that characterology may exist as a science some day, but that is still far off. This
is the least that one can say about it. Few psychologists will contradict
me if I assert that this "science" finds it quite hard to disengage itself
from the mists of philosophical eloquence and to enter the world of
number, measure and weight.

All these beautiful assertions on what occurs before and during
the conversion are gratuitous. In the actual state of the science *they
are at best only undecidables*. That is to say that on the one hand the
"science" can trace a plausible, provisional picture; the believer, on
the other hand, can recognize the sign of the invasion of divine grace
in the "accident." Until we have better information, we can only
analyze more and more precisely the characteristics of conversion:
an incubation very variable in its duration and its characteristics; a
release in circumstances that are also very variable, often in a religious edifice, or during the performance of a more or less religious
act, and *consequences* that are also very variable, manifesting themselves fully only many years after the appearance of the decisive
phenomenon. Finally, of course, the conversion can unfold in a very
progressive manner, in which the discursive and logical processes
take precedence over the affective. It is to be noted that here, as
always, I take the terms "discursive," "logical," "affective" *cum grano
salis*. Let us again repeat that I do not want to enclose myself in any
category whatsoever.

The study of conversion from within

We have just examined conversion in a purely descriptive manner
and from the outside. We can attempt an analysis of it from the
inside, even though it is a thousand times more difficult. What takes
place in the soul of the convert? In what does his difference of attitude
consist? Can it be explained in intellectualist terms? Not completely,
undoubtedly.

According to Abbé Girault's very apt expression the convert adheres to a "vague totality," the implications of which are sifted out little by little. I would say that after having studied the system from the outside, he discovers it suddenly from the inside, *he sees* "what it can be good for"; this "usefulness" immediately produces a general outlook which he, consciously or unconsciously, has never wanted to take. Sometimes this sudden comprehension lasts only as long as a lightning flash, but the whole of life is illumined by it. This profound change of attitude corresponds, I think, to the catastrophic phenomenon of conversion. It provokes a great surprise and a vivid emotion in the subject. It seems to him, probably quite justifiably— certainly for Catholics—that an external Influence has intervened to help him. I recall a convert whom I knew very well, who was tortured by the problem of evil and of suffering. This life, he thought, so beautiful, so rich, this exciting adventure, can come to an end at any moment by the invasion of death, sickness or madness. How can such a thought be borne? How could not all the joy in the world be dark- ened by it? Now, this man was a practicing and very convinced Catholic. His faith rested above all on metaphysical arguments and on family traditions, but it was enlightened. He did not ignore anything of the magnificent "chemistry of suffering" in the Christian religion, neither the communion of saints nor the redemptive role of suffering borne heroically. But he thought that these ideas were too beautiful for ordinary mortals, that they were the affair of saints whose minds perhaps were a bit feverish. *Finally it is all so theoretical,* without application to the ordinary man in contemporary life. But the cruel obsession which overwhelmed his soul drove him out of all the refuges of human wisdom. One afternoon of desperation, the sun shone on the happy countryside, but not for him. Then suddenly he saw the Christian synthesis (which, I repeat, he knew perfectly) in a new light: The brevity of life, compensated by eternal life, the necessity of complete renunciation, thought of the worth of each second, the value of sacrifice and of the acceptance of suffering which can save so many souls in an instant, if one really wants to. And Christ bearing his cross, asking him to cooperate in his work. "Poor soul, will you refuse as you have done until now?" Then his eyes opened and he recognized him; he "played the game"; he discovered the immense depth of familiar notions, unconsciously rejected from his motivation. There was no vision in this, no paranormal phenomenon. Everything was summed up in the change of moral attitude, sudden and definitive, and in the calmness that is finally found in the only harbor at the center of the sea of anxieties.

The preparatory techniques to conversion

All Christians believe that conversion does not depend on a simple effort of will and understanding, but also on divine assistance which God accords when he judges it good. However, they also believe that one must cooperate with grace, that is to say *adopt the suitable attitude,* which will allow God—if he wishes—to give the final help. We suppose therefore a sufficient knowledge of dogma. We also suppose the completion of the intellectual purification, which makes one clearly perceive the emptiness of so many pseudoproblems and the fragility of so many alleged obstacles. But these are only preliminaries. In order to arrive at the fundamental experience, a special technique is necessary, as always, which the old religious authors knew perfectly without defining it as we do in the twentieth century. It is here that we will see the ancient texts bloom again and certain sentences become clear in a mysterious light, like a theorem whose meaning and interest one suddenly grasps. But here the apprentice is hardly engaged upon his task when he runs into a preliminary difficulty. In order to observe the effects of the religious experience, one must have already felt them. How can they be felt before the religious experience begins? Let us not minimize the obstacle, it is enormous and at the base of a host of misunderstandings. We have to study a phenomenon which has not yet appeared in the field of consciousness, and to observe the effects of communication with God when this communication has not yet been established. This is painfully contradictory.

It is here, fellow scientist, that I request a moment of confidence, in the name of the many hours that we have spent together in the laboratory. Take exactly the mental attitude that I shall point out to you. At the end of a certain period of time, a series of phenomena will transpire, if your technique is correct—and above all if God wills it. . . .

a) First, eliminate from your life all deviations opposed to that which you seek. All religions insist that the experiment can only be set up in a pure heart. That is to say that all the moral errors enumerated by the Decalogue, and which all religions more or less repeat, must be carefully corrected. The reason for it is simple: conversion, in the etymological sense, consists in turning the gaze of the spirit toward an aspect of phenomena which one has not previously considered. Hence it is necessary to rouse in oneself an *interest* in this new aspect. Now, too sensual a life, hate, envy, love of money or honors etc. diminish this interest. For a scientist this is not a matter for discussion, it is an experimental fact. All the religious minds, all the mystics have stressed this. They are trained technicians, and they must be listened to.

The life of the scientist has its own asceticism, that is to say that the powerful interest brought to scientific experiments gradually consumes other activities. Like that of creators, their life becomes severely regulated by the cadence of their scientific occupations. The additional and methodical effort at purification will undoubtedly cause but slight hardship, once the necessity for it is understood.

b) It is now necessary to nourish the new interest that is aroused by religious phenomena. To know that there exists an immense literature in which the most profound and subtle minds, the most heroic souls, have in the course of centuries summed up the report of their experiences. The best way is to study the religious experience, in its purest and most intense expression, namely, among the saints. There are numerous lives of saints, unfortunately often of little value both from the literary and scientific view. Or perhaps they are too technical, written by scientific hagiographers not at all concerned about making themselves readable. But still it is not impossible to find accounts of experiences lived by saints. They must be read closely, paying careful attention to the *modifications of behavior* which a lived faith involved for these people of genius. Note also the considerable increase of *activity*, which becomes devouring in the majority of cases; the *energy* which develops to the point of retreating neither before sickness, nor torture, nor death. And also the very interesting phenomenon of *enormous influence* which the saint exercises on those around him. Nor must the ultimate phenomena be forgotten, which appear in cases such as St. Teresa or St. John of the Cross. They are rare and the immense majority of men have few chances of ever arriving at such heights. But these shining personalities are like the unknown corpuscle whose trajectory, once, by chance, condensed the gas in a Wilson Chamber. This led to the discovery of the meson and to new progress in atomic physics.

c) So far nothing does violence to the habitual logic of the sciences. But it is necessary to go further: The religious experience not being purely intellectual, one must live it and not content oneself with imagining it . . . We suppose an aroused interest. Suppose also that you are not ready to grant that saints are truly singular personages, not just psychopaths. Something must have driven them, but it is not clear what. One further step is necessary. One must begin to pray. I know to what extent such a suggestion may seem absurd. How is one to pray to a being whose existence one doubts? But there are certain forms of conditional imploration which do not shock reason too much. One can, for example, think of a Mind which governs matter and ask him, if it has a personal form, to send the light which may "enlighten every man coming into the world." One can imagine him as existing rather than as nonexisting, and even try to represent him to oneself in the form of the God of the Christians. Do not confuse the revolt of the old habits of thought with a revolt of reason in the strict sense. On a strict rational plane, in the narrowest sense of that term, I will grant that one can never prove the existence of God, if it be conceded to me that neither *can his nonexistence be proved.* Consequently, at this point, it would not be more irrational to test one hypothesis rather than another, since here we are engaged, not in a rational demonstration, but in an experimental verification.

Let us therefore test the God-hypothesis, but let us really test it, without cheating, that is to say by setting the theotropic function in motion again, undoubtedly atrophied by nonuse. For this, it is necessary to recall a truth familiar to Asia, but which young Western world too often ignores: one can do all kinds of exercises with one's mind, change its inclinations, increase its penetration or its attention, exactly as a gymnast progressively exercises his muscles and makes them capable of prowesses that would have been impossible at the beginning. Everybody in the West admits this ability in the realm of physical culture, but nobody believes it or thinks about it in terms of the psychic sphere. It is neither more or less easy in the one or the other case, and certainly one is not successful in one stroke. Everything depends on the perseverance shown in overcoming the little difficulties at first, then the greater ones involved in stressing the disadvantages of what one loves, and the advantages of what one does not yet love. Believe me, this is possible. I learned it once at my own expense during the course of a terrible journey along the icy banks of reason. I either had to find myself or perish. . . .

For the mental exercise, as always, the technique must be considered. The atmosphere is of the greatest importance. Holy and secluded places, the muffled music of the organ under ancient vaults, semidarkness, the sweet fragrance of incense—here are stimuli, more powerful than you can believe, which will help in re-awakening the theotropic function. But above all else, choose *silence:* God does not let himself be heard in agitation of the heart or the tumult of crowds. Consume only a limited quantity of these pious ingredients at the beginning. Do not force your tastes except with moderation. Above all, thought must not be inert. One must repeat mentally without tiring: God, if you exist, send me light, have pity on me. One must habituate himself without let-up to the system of thought that one would experience.

d) The last stage depends on Another. After months or years, if the good will has been great enough and the good faith perfect, if purification has been sufficiently pursued, if the interest has shifted away from the thing of the world and, perhaps, if suffering mixes its cruel but powerful aid with it, then something is produced. This system which up to now was seen only from the outside, with a desire to believe in it without being able to do so, is suddenly seen from the inside. One discovers *what it can be good for,* one sees its force, tolerance, efficacity, and one understands why the saints are invincible. And, even if this lasts but an instant, one cannot forget the source, one understands what must be understood.

Men have lived on this experience of a lightning flash all their lives, with a force and clarity that we hardly imagine. These heroes, these titans, our own "jivan muktas," are the saints of the West. It is in thinking about them, in attempting to follow their path from the beginning that we will better understand the *mystical experience.*

7

Mystical Experience

All that I have just described still belongs only to a rather modest level of religious experience. They are just "tests" which everyone can run without leaving the domain of "elementary physics." But in order to understand the science well, it is important to verify its results in the hands of the greatest. It is likewise with the theotropic function. What happens when it is in some way pushed to its culminating point? With what intensity does the process of experimental verification then work?

In order to combine a more ample knowledge with the most refined techniques, one must meet the saints. I am afraid that many scientists have never asked themselves about these curious personages. I would wager that for the majority of my fellow biologists the saints are but a curious variety of madmen or hysterics, unworthy of consorting with "the readers of graduations" as Eddington says. To the sceptics, I shall recall only that scientific honesty presupposes a preliminary and careful documentation before any judgment. And I shall ask what they have read on the subject. Since I am very much afraid that their information is most rudimentary I propose that they try a little journey into hagiography tailored to their taste. It will not be too long and perhaps not as boring as they might believe.

What if we begin with the most difficult, with the most hotly debated, with the great mystics? But let us immediately clarify the problem, by addressing ourselves directly *to the greatest,* like St. Teresa of Avila and St. John of the Cross. For if I do not believe that mystics are mad, there are nevertheless numerous cases of mystical madness. Among the lesser mystics one can find all the transitions, and certain of them possess only a grain of true mysticism dissolved in an ocean of monomania. The fact is that attempts at direct communication with the divine are *dangerous*. The adept is like the gymnast, who risks overexerting himself or breaking a limb if he is not supervised by an expert. But here the risks are more serious: Death and madness lie in wait for him who has overestimated his strength. Perhaps honest men have always known this, and it is this which would account for the union, general among primitive peoples, of the two notions of *the sacred* and *the dangerous*. In any case, Christians and Hindus do not ignore this, and their sacred books are full of severe admonitions to those who embark on this perilous path. Many have not paid heed, or did not have the required dispositions; their corpses are strewn along the route. These dangers are easily explained when one knows the goal that the great mystics very consciously wanted to attain. But it is so astonishing, it seems so extravagant at first sight, that it is best to disclose it only by degrees. Let us then first examine the practices of the ascetic drawn along the narrow path, tread by only a very few who managed to keep their courage.

The techniques of communication

The attempts to which I have alluded are as old as humanity, as we have seen, and belong to all religions, sometimes even to the most crude. But they are fully developed only in the great religions: Christianity, Hinduism and Islam. Thus we believe that it is more useful to grasp the phenomenon at its maximum of intensity, rather than decipher its original rudiments with difficulty. On the other hand, I prefer to address myself to the Christian religion in which a considerable quantity of first hand documents are directly available.

The mystics belong to all social environments, from the most refined like St. Francis, to the most rustic like St. Benedict Labre. The system of ideas, the personal problems which led them to orient themselves toward God are extremely varied. It is very difficult to give a sketch of it during a rapid summary like ours. The orientation is sometimes very precocious and takes place from early childhood. On the contrary it also happens (as with St. Ignatius) that it waits until the beginnings of maturity, generally after a more or less grave crisis. The change of life then reflects, as in conversion, the whole variety of temperaments.

In all cases the Christian traverses, or has already traversed, all the preliminary phases which I have discussed previously. Passions are corrected, the most serious faults attacked ardently. God is "taken seriously," who enters into all decisions, and thoughts dwell on God with increasing frequency. But most Christians stop here.

Certain souls derive only an increased "unsatisfaction" from all this and would like to go further. Sometimes they seek gropingly and for a very long time. But all Christians admit that this search is not vain, and that a higher assistance sooner or later leads it to its goal. Most often it is a question of meeting a guide, because the ascetics who get beyond the first stages of the journey are quite rare. This undoubtedly will astonish scientists whom life's afflictions might lead to trouble themselves about these problems: the mystical path has been carefully marked out, its dangers are perfectly known, sure and prudent guides have staked it out through many centuries. And this not only among the Hindus, as many believe, basing their knowledge on a very unequal literature, but also among Christians. In short, the technique is perfected, as in a treatise on physics, due allowance being made. First, the purgation of passions must be pursued with an ever-increasing rigor. Motivation will center itself on God, by abandoning all the purely human reasons for action, even the most licit. Asceticism is indispensable; restrictions on nourishment: St. Ignatius recommends the determination of just the right amount of nourishment necessary to attend to one's duties, and that nothing more than this ever be taken under any pretext; restrictions on the sexual life which, at least among laymen, does not necessarily go as far as the Hindu Brahmacharins. Contacts with the profane world are broken off or reduced to a minimum. The aim of all these practices is to strengthen *attention* and *will,* as many sacred authors declare explicitly. Finally, and above all, the practice of meditation and prayer is developed without respite. There are a thousand forms adapted to the most diverse circumstances and temperaments, and I can summarize only the essential points of the innumerable treatises which among Christians take the place of the *Upanishads* and *Puranas.* Perhaps, if it were necessary to summarize everything in a sentence, one could say that Christian prayer consists in doing the will of God. That is to say to represent him to oneself with ever-increasing intensity as the Creator, perfectly good and wise, as the sovereign aim of activity which must be purged of all personal inclination. At this stage it is necessary to forget oneself completely, to forget even the desire for heaven and the fear of hell. Here, in fact, desire and fear are no longer fitting, though they suffice for less advanced Christians. If one may employ a phrase which is not Christian, "our God is not the God of those people." Not that it is necessary to deny heaven or hell, but only because the entirely disinterested love of God must become the only motive. The Christian ascetic acts for love of the sublime goal toward which all his efforts tend, not out of the desire for reward or fear of punishment. He has changed his motivation while completely adhering to the same morality as the whole Christian people. We have moreover discussed the theory of stages on several occasions. Each one, going toward the same goal, chooses the motives which he finds efficacious, but he must exert himself to go higher. In pursuit of the truly pure and motivationally disinterested act, the only one agreeable to God, the ascetic will flee from himself. He renounces his own will and habituates himself to performing the most disagreeable acts without disgust and even with pleasure, if he believes them to conform with the divine will. This will is transmitted to him by the Christian education which he has received, and, in case of uncertainty, by the authorized interpreters of Scripture and tradition. It is in this sense that the vow of obedience pronounced by the religious must be interpreted. The superior is then the image of God on earth, and to obey him without hesitation and without a murmur then becomes but a means of renouncing one's own will.

Motivation is purified during the course of meditations increasingly deepened, where it is gently, but with an inflexible determination, rooted in the major themes of Christian thought: the infinite goodness of God, who loves men with an infinite love; infinite beauty, sovereignly worthy to be the center of all drives; rejection of the world insofar as it inspires sin, but acceptance of the world once it is purified. The effort is pursued without let-up and intense ordeals undergone for years (the "dark night" of which St. John of the Cross speaks). The psychic structure then re-organizes itself amidst the deepest anxiety, and prepares to go another step forward. When the faithful soul has heroically trained itself, it arrives at that point where great discoveries are made by always thinking about them: it thinks always of God.

The approach of the end

The moment has come to ask what do all these strenuous efforts, this perfect renunciation, this so minute preparation tend to? What does the mystic want? The reply is disconcerting and we shall have a first idea of it by listening to the poor and great al-Hallaj, the celebrated Moslem mystic sing, "O Guide of the ecstatics, I know Thee . . . Above all the concepts of those who have known thee, O my God, thou knowest me powerless to offer thee the thanksgiving due thee. Come then into me in order to thank thyself. This is the true thanksgiving, there is no other. I have become Him whom I love and Him who I love has become me, we are two spirits fused in a same body."

Before that, Plotinus had already said; "The spirit must first detach itself from bodily fetters, passions and sensible representations, this is *catharsis*. Then it must reduce all differences in its intelligence. It then becomes similar to the One and arrives at the very source of life." It is the famous "flight of the solitary to the Sole" *Phuge monou pros Mónon.*

St. John of the Cross was to say the same: "The substance of this soul, while not being substance of God because it cannot substantially change itself in him, yet united with him, absorbed in him, is God by the participation of God." *(Lama de amor viva).*

Finally, Alvarez de Paz *(De inquisitione pacis)*, "Thus aided and fortified, the spirit sees God. It does not arrive there by denying to, or by withdrawing something from, him, as when one says: God is neither limited or fixed. It is not either by regarding the divine grandeur without admixture, in the tranquillity of a serene day. Certainly, Oh reader, when you see the light with the eyes of the body, you do not arrive there by the association of ideas . . . You simply see the light. Likewise, in this degree of contemplation the soul asserts nothing, denies nothing, attributes nothing, discards nothing, but in full repose it sees God. One will say to me that this is astonishing or incredible rather . . . I confess that it is astonishing. Yet the fact is very certain."

You have read quite correctly. In the face of the vulgar who declare they "believe nothing except what they see" and who consequently deny God, a handful of mystics rises to declare that one can see God and lose oneself in him to the extent of losing one's own personality. On this the agreement between all mystics, from Plotinus to Ramakrishna through St. John of the Cross and St. Teresa, is absolutely striking. It seems that the humanity has always believed in this superhuman ambition, this desperate attempt, this open door to the Other World. It has always thought that it could escape toward the Elsewhere. And despite all deviations, despite the rarity of the successes, there have always been explorers around to try their luck. It is at this moment that the astonished scientist must push his inquiry further: Having arrived at the end what do the great mystics see? And what is the practical value of their testimony?

What the ascetic sees of that which the soul communicates

Let us suppose that a time machine transports us a thousand years ahead, and that one places in our hands a small pamphlet summarizing the state of physics of that time. We will not understand very much in it. And if the machine wildly pushed us on a hundred thousand years further—assuming that science has kept pace accordingly—the results of these times, the formulas that would then express the march of the universe would be radically unintelligible . . . Thus it can be foreseen that if the ascetic arrives at contemplating the Prime Mover of evolution, the goal toward which it tends, either his mind will be too feeble to embrace it, or his language will forever find it impossible to make us conceive it. For the road stretches too far ahead, and the light radiated by the Omega point, as Teilhard de Chardin says, renders all our concepts fuzzy.

Now, we encounter this precise difficulty of self-expression as the mystics. In this connection a passage from Angela de Foligno, which she dictated to her confessor, is completely characteristic: "And I saw God . . ." And like me, the scribe asked how, or what thing she saw, or if she saw a bodily thing? She answered thus, "I saw a plenitude, a clarity, of which I felt such a fullness that I cannot express and that I can compare to naught else. And I know not how to tell you that I saw a bodily thing. But it was like it is in heaven, namely a beauty so great that I can say naught to you save that it is only beauty and all good." And the saint despaired of what the scribe had noted down because, she said, that in no wise corresponded to what she wanted to express. This powerlessness of language to translate the inexpressible precisely has inspired the most beautiful passages in St. Teresa and St. John of the Cross. It is here that the mystical metaphors come in, borrowed from the vocabulary of human love in its most burning aspect. These metaphors are very frequent in the vocabulary of the great mystics, and they will shock only a reader seeking to see in them something other than unsuccessful attempts to say what cannot be said.

But then if we cannot understand the nature of the experience that the great mystics have undergone, how are we to judge it? By still following the rule of human experiment, namely *by its effects*. If somewhere, in some moment of time, some adventurous explorers have broken through the forbidden door and brought back treasures, it is on the objective plane that their value must be reckoned. What do they do with these treasures? What use do they make of this divine vision in which they have participated? Now, what do we see? The *greatest* mystics are like the ornaments of our species of which mankind preserves a heartstirring memory. The footsteps of St. Francis still resound in Asissi and in our hearts, despite the centuries. St. Teresa of Avila is one of the greatest writers in the Spanish language. And who does not admire the somber lightning flashes that stud the works of St. John of the Cross? But also and above all, the life of these pioneers of the infinite generally overflows with a prodigious activity. For if at first, as St. Teresa observes, the vision of the divine light has the effect of awakening a desire for the death that will deliver us from the obstacle which is the body, at another time—when another step forward has been taken—the will of the ascetic will merge with that of God. Now God has willed the world and requires that one act in it in order to expel evil and sin.

It is then that the action of the mystic develops, according to laws that are proper to them: the establishment of religious orders despite all the difficulties encountered, works of charity, indefatigable preaching, etc. Why admire only Gandhi? We have a hundred of his quality. Let us add moreover that the mystic often acts through his presence alone. He does not even need to speak, he appears and that suffices. The most hardened man cannot refuse anything to an ascetic who completely lives his ideal: objections collapse and we see behavior automatically align itself with the model. Certain words, said with a certain accent are like an echo of a lost Homeland. And the conscience, obscurely, recognizes them, and conforms to them. From this point of view nothing is more interesting than the influence exercised on his parish by the saintly Curé d'Ars, a poor man whose intelligence was not brilliant. But one day he understood what was to be understood and he lived in a state of complete renunciation. And suddenly the boorish yokels of whom he was the pastor began to listen to him, and, what is more, do what he said!

Thus it is also with the *intelligence* they show in their writings; or better still with the *action* they exert on the moral world with a perseverance that nothing discourages; and most often by their mere presence. Here are arguments that tend to prove that what they have seen must be valid. But I wish still to stress one of their qualities, because this is especially pleasing to the man of the laboratory: this is their *scientific prudence*.

The term perhaps may astonish the ignorant who has never thought of saints otherwise than as annoying variety of deranged persons. In fact at first sight it appears that this intense concentration, this monomania which has only God as an object, leads most directly to the worst dangers and hallucinations and can completely derange the mind. Now, the Christian mystics have never been ignorant of this. We have already seen that they consider ecstasy as an annoyance, as a bodily weakness devoid of importance of which it is not seemly to boast, but which one must mistrust. Finally, a number of mystics, among the greatest, have ended by conjuring ecstasies and paranormal phenomena away, which they were very happy to do in general. Saintliness is not ecstasy, far from it. No matter how much such an assertion may, perhaps, astonish some, it must be solidly established.

Paranormal phenomena must be discarded

St. John of the Cross and Bañez were very distrustful of visions. Bañez even recommended that no attention be paid to them: if they come from God, they will be able to act without us. In connection with the *Life of St. Teresa* he wrote: "One point, however, quite

rightfully commands reserve so long as it will not have been subjected
to a serious examination: these are the revelations and visions which
this book presents in great number. These things are always to be
viewed with doubt, especially with women who are more inclined
than others to attribute them to God and to place saintliness there.
And yet it is not therein that saintliness exists." Far from contra-
dicting it, St. Teresa herself recommends great prudence to superiors:
"Neither must they imagine that because a sister has been favored by
graces of this kind she is better than the others." Later on she
recommended that nuns who were a bit too *exalteé* for her taste be
made to eat meat. "As regards Sister Saint Jerome, it will be
necessary to recommend that she eat meat for several days and be
kept away from her prayers. She has a feeble imagination, and she
believes she sees and hears everything that she tells me." Let us now
see St. John of the Cross, "It is necessary to know that if all these
effects that can be produced in our bodily senses have God as author,
one must never regard them with security or accept them. Rather it is
necessary to flee from them completely without even investigating
whether they proceed from a good or a bad principle. When the soul
sees itself the object of such extraordinary manifestations, it very
often thereby conceives a certain satisfaction with itself. And imagines
itself to be something before God. Now, this goes counter to humility.
The soul must never pretend to be pleased with these manifestations,
even if they were to come from God. For if the soul is pleased by them,
six disadvantages ensue therefrom: 1) The perfection of the faith
is lessened; 2) These communications are an obstacle for the spirit,
because the soul comes to a stop there and *the spirit does not take
its flight toward* the invisible; 3) Little by little the soul attaches a
proprietary sense to these communications; it does not walk along
the path of renunciation and spiritual destitution; 4) The soul
attaches itself to what is sensible, hence to what is of least importance;
5) The soul thereby little by little loses the favors of God; 6) When
the soul seeks these communications, it opens the door to the devil"
(*Ascent of Mt. Carmel* II, chap. XI).

St. Teresa moreover never positively believed that these things
came from God "in such a way as to be able to assert it under oath."
And she kept her mind free enough to describe the symptoms of

ecstasy in herself and others, "The body maintains the attitude in which it was seized: thus it rests standing or seated, the hands open or closed. Even though its movements are paralyzed, the sensations are not always abolished. One hears like a confused sound that comes from afar. At the highest degree, one does not see, feel, or hear anything. Even the consciousness of self can be lost, but this lasts a short time" (*Vida*).

It is therefore more astonishing to see authors, otherwise very distinguished ones like Leuba, assert that the depth of saintliness bears a relation to the intensity of the trance. This has never been the doctrine of the Church, quite the contrary. And as one sees the mystics themselves are extremely distrustful in this regard. The truly pure act and thought, truly turned only toward God: this is what the perfectly accomplished ascetic does, and naught else.

The mystics have not limited themselves to stressing the dangers of any attachment whatsoever to the aberrant phenomena that they encountered on their path. In a host of treatises which cannot be summarized here, they wanted to minutely stake out and trace the path of correct meditation. Since the earliest times, they precisely pointed out its *nonconcrete character*. Evagrius Ponticus, the master of Greek spirituality, had already declared, "Wishing to see the face of the heavenly father, during your prayers do not force yourself to discern some image or figure. Flee the desire to see angels, powers or Christ in sensible form, otherwise you risk to fall into madness." And why is it fitting to abstain from doing so? For the reason that attention and the will are enormously strengthened in meditation and because one can see what one wishes to see. I knew a beginner who found it advantageous to concentrate on the Tabernacle and to imagine the divine Power floating above it like a cloud, spreading its shadow over the faithful in prayer. Soon the cloud assumed too much importance in his mind and he felt it envelop his meditation. But something unknown and evil seemed to him to be crouched in the center of it. So he rid himself of the image of the cloud, in order to address himself to God alone, without the intermediary of a material figure, even a vague one. And he felt the better for it. As Evagrius said, it is the contemplation of the divinity itself which constitutes the only aim of the effort of ascetics. Any object lower than the pure and *immaterial* divinity, angel or even Christ himself, would be an obstacle to the final aim.

The mystics and the Church

It seems to me that the greatest mystics of the West have always been in accord with the Church. Maréchal and Catholic authors agree. While paying homage to the great effort of objectivity that Delacroix and different nonbelieving critics make, it seems to me that they do not clarify the problem by considering at one and the same time all the personages who have advanced far, or who have claimed to, along the mystical path. This would be the equivalent of studying physics by placing on the same plane all the physics books written for amateurs or professionals, which one would find in a same country. It is necessary to sort things out. In the presence of such astonishing and rare phenomena, should we not investigate those who have declared themselves to be their bearers? If they reveal themselves in current life (that is to say in the domain of the verifiable) as sage persons leading an irreproachable life, one would find himself more inclined to trust them than if the opposite is true.

Now this is just what the Church very prudently does in the presence of mystics. She judges them by their works, according to that precept of the Gospel which would have the tree judged by its fruits. In the words of Deuteronomy: "If you say to yourselves, 'How can we recognize an oracle which the Lord has spoken?', know that even though a prophet speaks in the name of the Lord, if his oracle is not fulfilled or verified, it is an oracle which the Lord did not speak. The prophet has spoken it presumptuously, and you shall have no fear of him" (Dt. 18: 21-22). We again find the old criterion of works, of action on the external world, which so deeply characterizes the West. Its mystics are themselves deeply marked by the seal of action, as even Leuba observes.

But once the sorting out is effected, the Church places her great mystics on her altars, she recognizes them as saints, she bestows on them the title of doctor, as with St. John of the Cross. They themselves manifest a filial attachment to the Church, suffering with her, making her preoccupations theirs, intervening actively in her affairs (like St. Catherine of Siena). As a matter of fact, theologians are wont to discuss the claims of seeing God in this life which every mystic makes. And they ask themselves whether this could pertain to the *beatific vision* which shall be our portion in the other life. St. Thomas was not absolutely against such a privilege, but he restricted it to very exceptional cases. On the other hand, some theologians, following the Augustinian tradition, are more favorable to such a view. The discussion (the details of which one can read in Maréchal) soon took too theoretical a turn for my taste. It is very difficult to decide between ascetics who assert with a unanimous voice to have undergone a certain experience, and theologians who think, without having undergone it, that it is not such as the former have described it. Let us content ourselves, without going into further detail, with believing that the mystical experience comes as near to God as human nature, with the aid of grace, can. Moreover we must not forget the assertion of all the mystics that nature, relying on its own powers, is radically incapable of attaining God: it can only beat down the obstacles which oppose this encounter. It is God himself who, if he wishes, makes the rest of the journey.

Mystics and science

Here I would like to stick to the general plan of this book and avoid involvement with a host of controversies which lead nowhere. But nevertheless I cannot avoid breaking some lances over the backs of certain psychiatrists whose smug self-assurance annoys me to the highest degree. While they can express a rather poor opinion of mystics, many of their arguments do not at all have the force they think they have, because of the shabby state of psychiatric "science" itself. Biologists or specialists in other sciences must not let themselves be taken in too much by the doctors of the deranged. For, outside of neural physiology does psychiatry truly exist?

This is what many experimental psychologists, of which I am one, continue to ask themselves. It is almost fifty years now that psychology has emerged from a purely descriptive state, in which it had bogged down since its origin, in order to penetrate the domain of measure and the sciences. It immediately realized striking successes, and it would make even more if jealous psychiatrists did not do everything to forbid it entry to the hospitals. Psychiatry has remained in the rear. Many of its practitioners are twisted by the deplorable medical tradition, in which too-rapidly-drawn conclusions, hasty assimilations, and phraseology occupy too much place. They imagine that merely to classify deliriums is to advance very much in the comprehension of their mechanism. Having failed to effect its revolution, psychiatry has too often remained a conjectural science. Consequently we can view with a quizzical smile so many good people whose assertions are the more dogmatic the more their certainties are unconfirmed.

May I be excused for this outburst, but nothing irritates me more than pseudoscience, because it prevents the birth of true science. Getting back to the mystics, it is absolutely certain that many, even among the greatest, suffered from obsessions or different psychopathic illnesses. These diseases are, moreover, common among men of genius, and one must realize that saints are religious geniuses. But it is important to see well how they dominate their organism, how they make use even of obstacles to go forward. William James also suffered from anxiety neurosis which he valiantly fought against and over which he triumphed. Will one refuse to examine his philosophy because he was a psychopath? In a word then the work of the great mystics must be considered; their efficaciousness measured, still and always. It must also be noted that the preliminary training is dangerous (nobody is more conscious of this than they themselves), but it requires of them nothing that is absurd in itself. From the moment that one is convinced that a Supreme Reality infinitely transcends the face of this world, what is more reasonable than to concentrate one's attention on it in the hope of at last finding the passage? Narrow is the path leading there and surrounded with abysses into which many fall, even though they are as courageous as the greatest. But the precipices do not block off the path. In truth, these people are explorers. They have the boldness and spirit of adventure. Rather than seek to put impediments in their path, let us bring our sympathy to those who, perhaps, are ahead of everybody else, holding aloft the torch of the *élan vital*.

The Bergsonian position

At the end of my study, it is time to acknowledge everything I owe to my master, Bergson, and to his immortal book *The Two Sources of Morality and Religion*. I have been able only to summarize—too rapidly—some of the essential themes of Bergson's great work on religion, trying not to deform too much the thought of one of the greatest philosophers the twentieth century has produced.

His metaphysics in "The Two Sources" adopts the position of a scientist, an attitude which in my opinion is particularly fruitful and which I myself have tried to take in the course of this work: "A certain representation is built up *a priori*, and it is taken for granted this is the idea of God; from thence are deduced the characteristics that the world ought to show; and if the world does not actually show them, we are told that God does not exist. Now who can fail to see that if philosophy is the work of experience and reasoning, it must follow just the reverse method, question experience on what it has to teach us about a Being Who transcends tangible reality as He transcends human consciousness, and so appreciate the nature of God by reasoning on the facts supplied by experience? . . .

"It is also possible with Plato to lay down *a priori* a definition of the soul as a thing incapable of decomposition because it is simple, incorruptible because it is indivisible, immortal by virtue of its essence. This leads, by a process of deduction, to the idea of souls falling into Time, and thence to that of a return into Eternity. But what is to be the answer to those who deny the existence of that soul thus defined? And how could the problems touching a real soul, its real origin, its real fate, be resolved in accordance with reality, or even posited in terms of reality, when one has merely been speculating upon a possibly baseless conception of the soul, or at the very best, defining conventionally the meaning of the word which society has inscribed on a slice of reality, set apart for the convenience of conversation? . . . The Platonic conception has not helped our knowledge of the soul by a single step, for all that it has been meditated upon for two thousand years."[1]

For a very long time in fact, and still today, the ideal of the sciences and philosophy has been to resemble geometry and to proceed only by induction. Now, in the natural sciences and in modern psychology, *experiment, only experiment,* can guarantee the truth of the concepts. Of what use is the theory which does not work, which does not modify the real in the sense that one has foreseen? Those who claim to describe a lived experience deserve attention, provided that an ensemble of moral qualities guarantees their good faith and their objectivity, and at the same time their behavior and their activity appear to agree with the real.

Bergson in addition observes that in the course of evolution, life seems to want only the preservation of the species, and this is doubtlessly why each animal fights unflinchingly to find its food and a female, raise its offspring, and above all preserve life. In it, there is no need to want to live *consciously,* because there is nothing to show that it is thinking of death or conceiving it even at the moment it occurs, otherwise than in the form of violent but diffused anxiety. With man, on the contrary, reflection coils back upon itself, and death is envisaged even in a period of absolute security. But the idea of death leads to that of "What's the good of it?" and blocks the will to live. Then, says Bergson, an evolution which wants the machine to continue to turn must secrete the reasons to live which would fit the new type of conscious animal to which it is about to give birth: it is nothing else but the idea of the rewarding and provident God, the supreme aim of activity. *This or that man was not responsible for this discovery, but the species in general.* And what if this discovery corresponded to a turning of evolution upon itself, to a vision of an origin that at the same time a goal, to that Final Reason, the contemplation of which fills the heart of the mystic with an inexhaustible energy and opens the sources of life again in cataracts? The prelude, perhaps, to some new and unheard of accomplishment as the imposing dreams of a Teilhard de Chardin allow us to glimpse.

[1]Henri Bergson, *The Two Sources of Morality and Religion,* tr. by R. Ashley Audra and Claudesley Brereton (New York: Holt, 1935), pp. 250-51.

Glossary of Terms

VIA NEGATIONIS: a theological procedure through which, by recognizing the powerlessness of reason to determine what God is, one tries at least to establish what he is not, by successively removing all human limitations. It is almost like the "Neti . . . Neti" (not that, not that) of the Upanishads.

THURSTONE AND SPEARMAN: these scientists have attempted to sift out the factors that govern success in very varied psychological tests. This has led them to confirm the insufficiency of the classical divisions of the intellectual function, and to establish completely different ones.

FACTORIST ANALYSIS: the procedure employed by Thurstone, Spearman and their school. It consists of determining the correlations between the different tests by mathematical analysis. One can thereby establish what they have in common and the parts that vary in the same way. Also employed for determining the factors of success in tests.

PROPOSITIONAL LOGIC: one can so designate that modern part of logic which has abandoned philosophy in order to become a science. It rejects the use of current language, because it has been formed in a hazardous manner and without logic and because it can hamper thinking. The mathematico-logicians substituted symbols for it which are easier to handle and combine. A syllogism is then reduced to three or four signs.

DYAUS PITR: (shining sky-father) (from which Jupiter derives): the supreme God of the first Aryans.

ANTHROPOMORPHIC EXTRAPOLATION: said of that procedure of reasoning which consists in leading everything precipitately to human behavior, by going beyond the facts, without even taking them into account.

TROPISM: from Greek word which means "I turn," it designates the act of an animal which turns automatically toward a source of stimulation, for example, light. The observation of such phenomena led Loeb to think that everything can be reduced to tropism, even the very complex actions of higher animals.

THE MECHANISTIC SCHOOL: it explains everything by a series of simple and inductable mechanisms. Loeb is a strict mechanist.

ANOSMIC: the fact of being deprived of an olfactory sense.

COGNITIVE MAP: this expression of Tolman means that the animal can form a notion of the situation for itself in terms of a gratuitous knowledge, without it having any pressing problems to solve.

ANISOTROPIC STIMULATIONS: stimuli that are not uniformly distributed, coming from one side more than from another.

DRIVE: the great internal influences which incline toward this or that action (hunger, thirst, sexual appetite) are called drives.

S–R THEORISTS: strictly mechanistic theoreticians who are willing to admit only that stimulus S necessarily engenders reaction R.

HEDONIC: in a general sense pleasurable, or relating to pleasure.

MEASURE OF NERVOUS DISCHARGE: one can now, by implanting very fine electrodes in a nerve, record the miniscule electric currents that accompany nervous activity, and thereby obtain an external image of it.

OPINIONNAIRE: a type of questionnaire currently being used by experimental psychologists, in which the subject is asked to answer questions in writing.

NEOLITHIC AGE: the age of polished stone. It followed the Paleolithic age, characterized by the use of hewn stone. It was in the Neolithic age that modern man (*Homo sapiens*) definitively replaced the rougher type of Neanderthal man who lived in the Paleolithic age.

THE DOGONS: men who inhabit the cliffs of Bandiagara in Africa and show themselves, according to Griaule, of being possessed only by the concern of doing again to the least detail what was done by their mythical ancestors, whose deeds are remembered by the older folk, without which the act has no value, it does not succeed, and draws bad luck. Such an obsession annuls the possibility of reasoning and progress.

PRELOGICAL MENTALITY: a theory which Lévy-Bruhl particularly developed, according to which primitive peoples do not reason—or not yet—as we do. Their intellectual mechanisms are supposedly not in a state to function regularly and they would willingly admit, for example, contrary assertions.

SUMERIAN AND THE AKKADIAN CIVILIZATION: developed around the base of the Persian Gulf circa 3000 B.C., while civilizations of the time flourished approximately at the same time in the basin of Indus, at Harappa and Mohenjo Daro. They are the oldest civilizations that we know, anterior even to the ancient Egyptian empire, and nevertheless already very developed.

HADES: the hell of the Greeks in which the souls of the dead live in a state of semi-consciousness.

GENS: the Roman family: *numen* and *iuno*: a spirit who protects or animates either man or woman.

LEMURALIA: the feast of the dead.

"MANES EXITE PATERNI": ghosts of my fathers, leave!

LAO TSE: the great Chinese metaphysician, very different from Confucius who was in no way a metaphysician. His doctrine was not unrelated to those of India.

THE RABBIS: the doctors of law, indefatigable commentators and subtle interpreters. They were later to affix the enormous sum of their reflections to the Bible (*The Talmud*).

METEMPSYCHOSIS: a doctrine in particular favor in India, but not unknown to some ancient peoples like the Greeks. It postulates a series of purifying migrations of the soul after death, in a series of other beings, human or animal.

TARTARUS AND PHLEGETHON: in Greek mythology, rivers which irrigate the dwelling place of the dead.

PHALARIS: the tyrant of Agrigentum (circa 549 B. C.), who roasted voyagers alive in a brazen bull.

ELUSINIAN MYSTERIES: the secret religious rites of ancient Greece. At his initiation the adept of these mysteries pronounced more or less the following sentence: "I have fasted, I have drunk 'kukeon' (a special beverage), I have seized (the sacred objects) in the basket (kiste), I have handled them; I have put them in the 'kalathos' (receptacle)."

DAEMON: Socrates makes numerous allusions to his personal daemon who supports and advises him. This does not seem to be a mere figure of speech.

ESCHATOLOGY: designation for the hope in a world or an event to come, in relation to which one orients all his acts.

UPANISHADS: with the Vedas and the Puranas (commentaries) they form part of the enormous series of holy scriptures of India. There are several Upanishads (Chandogya, Brihandaranyaka—Upanishad, etc. (1) The most ancient traditions are expressed in the Vedas (Rig–Veda, Yayyur–Veda, Atharva Veda) which claim to go back to the creation of the world. The thinking of every good Hindu proceeds from the Vedas.

SAMKHYA, WITH THE VEDANTA: the principal Hindu philosophical systems.

KRISHNA: the blue God, the lover of shepherdesses, one of the most popular aspects of the divinity in all India. He serves as Arjuna's coachman in the Bhagavad—Gita.

CYMNOSOPHISTS (THE NAKED SAGES): terms by which the Greeks, struck by the ritual nudity of many sects of India, designated the Hindu sages.

RISHIKESH: a locality in Himalaya abounding in hermitages.

SADHAK: a student.

ASHRAN: the whole body of students who listen to the lectures of a sage.

DARK NIGHT OF THE SOUL: expression used by mystics to characterize the anxieties that follow the first purifications. Few mystics escape it: it involves a state of despairing tepidity, accompanied by a feeling of unworthiness and the futility of one's efforts. The soul "no longer feels God" and the discouraged adept thinks of suicide. The dark night can last very long and according to those learned in the mystical state it corresponds to a reorganization of the soul before the definite fusion in the divine life.

Bibliographical Sketch

The writings listed in this bibliography are meant to provide a random sampling of the vast literature in the diverse fields touched upon in this book. Almost any of the books listed herein contain a sufficient bibliography to put the interested reader well on his way into a particular field of inquiry.

Chapter 1

ANASTASIA, ANNE. *Differential Psychology. Individual and Group Differences in Behavior.* 3rd edition. New York: Macmillan, 1958.

BAYET, A. *La morale scientifique.* Paris: Alcan, 1905.

HOSTIE, RAYMOND. *Religion and the Psychology of Jung.* Translated by G. R. LAMB. New York: Sheed & Ward, 1957.

LeROY, EDOUARD. *Le problème de Dieu.* Paris: Cahiers de la Quinzaine, 1929.

MOUROUX, JEAN. *The Christian Experience. An Introduction to a Theology.* Translated by GEORGE LAMB. New York: Sheed & Ward, 1954.

STODDARD, G. D. *The Meaning of Intelligence.* New York: Macmillan, 1944.

STONE, CALVIN P. (ed.). *Comparative Psychology.* 3rd edition. New York: Prentice-Hall, 1951.

Chapter 2

Current Theory and Research in Motivation. A Symposium. Papers by JUDSON S. BROWN, HARRY F. HARLOW, LEO J. POSTMAN, VINCENT

Nowlis, Theodore M. Newcomb, O. Hobart Mowrer. Lincoln, Nebraska: University of Nebraska Press, 1953.

Dreger, R. M. "Some Personality Correlates of Religious Attitudes as Determined by Projective Techniques," *Psychological Monographs*, 66 (1952), 335.

Hilgard, Ernest R. *Theories of Learning.* 2nd edition. New York: Appleton-Century-Crofts, 1956.

Middleton, W. C. "Some Reactions toward Death among College Students," *Journal of Abnormal and Social Psychology*, 31 (1936), 165-71.

Munn, L. *Handbook of Psychological Research on the Rat.* Boston: Houghton Mifflin, 1950.

Nelson, E. S. P. "Patterns of Religious Shifts from College to Fourteen Years Later," *Psychological Monographs*, 70 (1956), 1-15.

Stacey, G. L. and Reichen, M. L. "Attitudes towards Death and Future Life among Normal and Subnormal Adolescent Girls," *Exceptional Children*, 20 (1954), 259-62.

Thouless, R. H. "The Tendency to Certainty in Religious Belief," *British Journal of Psychology*, 26 (1935), 16-31.

Chapter 3

Eliade, Mircea. *Le chamanisme et les techniques archaïques de l'extase.* Paris: Payot, 1949.

———. *Patterns in Comparative Religion.* Translated by Rosemary Sheed. New York: Sheed & Ward, 1958.

Frazer, James G. *The Golden Bough.* Abridged edition. New York: Macmillan, 1922.

Harrison, Jane E. *Prolegomena to the Study of the Greek Religion.* 3rd edition. New York: Meridian, 1955.

Hastings, James (ed.). *Encyclopaedia of Religion and Ethics.* 16 vols. New York: Scribner's, 1908-1927.

Le Bras, G. *Eléments de sociologie religieuse.* 2 vols. Paris: Presses Universitaires, 1956.

SCHMIDT, WILHELM. *Ursprung des Gottesidee.* 12 vols. Münster in Westphalia: Aschendorff, 1912-1955.

Chapter 4

LHERMITTE, J. *Le miracle.* Paris: Gallimard, 1956.

THURSTON, HERBERT. *The Physical Phenomena of Mysticism.* Edited by J. H. CREHAN. Chicago: Regnery, 1952.

Chapter 5

Bhagavad-gita; the Song of God. Translated by SWAMI PRABHAVAN-ANDA and CHRISTOPHER ISHERWOOD. With an Introduction by ALDOUS HUXLEY. Hollywood: Rodd, 1944.

ELIADE, MIRCEA. *Le Yoga. Immortalité et liberté.* Paris: Payot, 1954.

HERDERT, S. *Spiritualité hindoue.* Paris: Michel, 1947.

MUELLER, F. MAX (ed.). *The Sacred Books of the East.* 50 vols. Oxford: Clarendon, 1879-1910.

ROUGEMENT, D. DE. *L'aventure occidentale de l'homme.* Paris: Michel, 1957.

COPLESTON, FREDERICK. *A History of Philosophy.* Vol. I, *Greece and Rome.* Westminster, Maryland: Newman, 1948.

Chapter 6

AIGRAIN, R. *L'hagiographie.* Paris: Bloud & Gay, 1953.

GILILAND, A. R. "The Attitude of College Students towards God and the Future Life," *Journal of Social Psychology,* 2 (1940), 18.

GIRAULT, R. "Le présentation du message chrétien." Unpublished thesis, Institut Catholique de Paris, 1948.

HARMS, E. *Psychologie und Psychiatrie der Konversion.* Leiden, 1924.

NEDONCELLE, M. and GIRAULT, R. *J'ai recontré le Dieu vivant.* Paris: Revue des Jeunes, 1952.

SANCTIS, S. DE. *La converzione religiosa.* Bologna, 1924.

VETTER, C. B. and GREEN, M. "Personality and Group Factors in the Making of Atheists," *Journal of Abnormal and Social Psychology*, 27 (1932), 179-94.

Chapter 7

BERGSON, HENRI. *The Two Sources of Morality and Religion.* Translated by R. ASHLEY AUDRA and CLAUDESLEY BRERETON. New York: Holt, 1935.

DELACROIX, H. *Les grands mystiques chrétiens.* Paris: Alcan, 1938.

MARECHAL, J. *Études sur la psychologie des mystiques.* 2 vols. Tournay: Desclée de Brouwer, 1937-1938.

WALSH, WILLIAM THOMAS. *Saint Teresa of Ávila. A Biography.* Milwaukee: Bruce, 1943.